T0323908

Demystifying

Creativity

This book is a study of the psychology, neuroscience, and philosophy of creativity, originality, and inspiration viewed from the lens of a seasoned game developer. It introduces the concept of creative sobriety—a practice that advocates better understanding our own sources of inspiration so that we can intellectually drive our creative voice closer to originality.

The creative process is an improvised dance between the conscious and the subconscious mind, where knowledge, experience, intuition, observation, imagination, and projection meet in ways that are completely unique to each person. Presenting practical and theoretical approaches to originality and game concept generation, this book explores the notion of creative sobriety before moving to chapters that blend theory and practice, covering topics such as innovation, the creative process, auteurship, collaboration, and creative vision.

This book will be of great interest to students of game design and creative professionals working within the industry as well as those looking to learn more about the creative process.

Fawzi Mesmar is an award-winning creative director, game designer, leader, author, and public speaker who has been in the gaming industry for more than two decades. His career has spanned the Middle East, New Zealand, Japan, and Europe, working for companies such as Ubisoft, EA, Activision Blizzard, Gameloft, and Atlus to name a few. He has worked on more than 20 titles that have been enjoyed by millions of players worldwide, including entries in the *Mario + Rabbids*, *Battlefield*, and *Star Wars* franchises.

Demystifying
Creativity

On Originality in
Game Development

Fawzi Mesmar

CRC Press
Taylor & Francis Group
Boca Raton London New York

CRC Press is an imprint of the
Taylor & Francis Group, an **informa** business

Cover design: Yasser Abu-Al Thurayya
Graphics: Ahmed Salama
Photo: Hanna Fogelberg

First edition published 2025
by CRC Press
2385 NW Executive Center Drive, Suite 320, Boca Raton FL 33431

and by CRC Press
4 Park Square, Milton Park, Abingdon, Oxon, OX14 4RN

CRC Press is an imprint of Taylor & Francis Group, LLC

ISBN: 9781032200057 (hbk)
ISBN: 9781032200033 (pbk)
ISBN: 9781003261834 (ebk)

DOI: 10.1201/9781003261834

Typeset in Helvetica
by codeMantra

For Hatem Mesmar,
who left us before he got the chance to read this.
Thanks for everything, dad.

Contents

Foreword

Translated from Japanese
Hello readers,

My name is Hiromasa Iwasaki.

My friend Fawzi asked me to write the Foreword for this book, and I decided to accept the offer because I thought it would be a great honor.

First, I would like to introduce myself to you, the readers.

I am a veteran of the video game industry, having started in 1988. I am still active in the video game industry. And these days, I don't see anyone older than me in most companies.

I work most of the time as a game designer and programmer.

My most famous work is *Ys Book 1 & 2* for the TurboGrafx 16 CD-ROM.

Other well-known games in Japan are *Tengai Makyo II*, *Linda Cube* and *Emerald Dragon* from the PC Engine era, but these games were not localized for the western market, so they are not very well known. I was also surprised to learn from Fawzi that *NAtURAL DOCtRINE* is also known in Europe and the United States, so I guess it is another one of my creations.

My Little Pony: Friendship is Magic, published by Gameloft, is my biggest success on mobile. The lead game designer for this game was Mr. Fawzi, so it was our biggest hit together.

I have also been a game journalist since 1985 and have over 10 years of experience reviewing games for game magazines. With this experience, I have now made it my life's work to preserve the development history of mainly Japanese Hudson and Falcom games.

I have worked as a programmer, game designer, creative director, game studio manager, and company executive for almost 40 years, but what I love most is still making games. Life is short, and the number of games you can make in a lifetime is small. So, making games is the most fun. That is why I am currently working as both lead game designer and lead programmer for one game.

Now that I have briefly introduced myself, how did I meet Fawzi? Fawzi and I met at the Gameloft New Zealand studio in 2011. The first time he impressed me was when Fawzi requested a meeting with me.

It was a complaint that he was an experienced game designer but was not being treated as he deserved for his skills. So, I remember telling him that I would put him to work on a proper project right away.

At the time, I thought he was a noticeably confident game designer, but then I saw his work and realized what a great game designer he was. He loved games, had played an enormous number of games, had a vast knowledge of games, and had a solid knowledge of ideas and mechanics. He also used that knowledge well, and his ideas were brilliant. He also had a sense of humor, which I think is necessary for a lead game designer. Unfortunately, when we are working on a game, it is often the case that our team is put in a tough situation due to deadlines and all sorts of other reasons. At such times, if the leader looks serious and pained, the morale of the team members will suffer. Therefore, it is at such times that the leader must put on a nonchalant face and inspire the morale of the team with a humorous attitude. Humor is also important to prevent the leader from delegitimizing others when he or she becomes angry.

So, I think humor is absolutely necessary for a leader. And Fawzi had a sense of humor. In other words, he had what it takes to be a leader in tough times.

He was also good at teaching people.

In other words, he was a great game designer who had what it takes.

So, he quickly became the principal game designer at the studio and engaged in a lot of hit games.

And about 2 years after I came back to Japan, he also came to Japan for a vacation.

Of course, I met him, and he told me that he was thinking of changing jobs.

I immediately invited him to join the Japanese company I was working for at the time, and to my surprise, he joined, and we were able to work together.

At that time, I was a board member of the company, and I wanted to make the company's game production system more like a Western studio, so I asked Fawzi to help me, but unfortunately, the cultural difference between Japan and the West was too big, and it didn't take off. And just before I left that company in 2016, he left as well, and he went back to Europe and became a studio director at KING.

He then went on to work at DICE, UBI, etc., while I kept in touch with him and ended up writing the Foreword to his book.

So finally, I would like to introduce this book.

This book is Fawzi's insight into creativity and inspiration.

He defines what creativity and inspiration are from the words of historical figures, the results of modern medical science, etc. and discusses how important they are to art and science, how they can be nurtured, and how they can be evaluated from multiple perspectives. This book also offers multiple perspectives on the meaning of creativity.

It also discusses how insight, or the sudden clarity of understanding of complex problems and ideas, is closely related to creativity, using the same historical figures and medical research to explain its importance and the relationship between creativity and the arts, sciences, and other fields. It is a book about creativity and its relationship to the arts, sciences, and other fields.

In short, it is a book that takes on the great challenge of describing the full range of aspects of human creativity, something that AI does not have today and will be hard to have in the future.

I really enjoyed reading it.

So, dear readers, are you ready to embark on a journey of creativity? Off you go!

Hiromasa Iwasaki
Creative Director / Game Designer / Creator YS Series
Tokyo, Japan
June 2024

Acknowledgments

This book wouldn't have been possible without the initial spark of inspiration of observing Stephen Jarret's initiatives to activate and lead central design when we worked together at Activision Blizzard King, our conversations on analogous inspiration ended up inspiring me to look into the matter further and lead to my initial hypotheses that I went on to validate with students and design teams I worked with since. Thanks also to Tomasz Kaczmarek and Eric Zimmerman, who encouraged me to put those thoughts and theories on paper for the first time.

Lots of other inspiration come from discussions on creativity and art that I had with Jac Carlsson, Manuel Llanes, Yasmeen Ayyashi, and Magda Chołyst; their views on design, music, and dance were deeply captivating. Conversations with Celia Hodent who gave me valuable insights and resources on psychology and neuroscience of creativity.

I am also grateful for the support and trust that I received from Shila Vikström, who helped me so much during the final stretch of the ride and was instrumental to me finishing this thing on time.

I also need to thank all of the friends and family who helped in reading the different drafts and manuscripts and provided me with constant feedback: Feras Musmar, Hannes Lidbeck, Sud Abbas, Johanna Pirker, Valeria Rossi, Afonso Ferreira, Rami Ismael, Osama Dorias, Jenny Xu, Erik Ortman, Patric Nordmark, and Melissa Abecassis.

Thank you so much to the trust and support of my editor and partner-in-crime Will Bateman, to Ahmed Salama for helping me with the graphs in this book and to Yasser Abu Al-Thurayya for the design of the cover.

As always, I am forever grateful to my mentor Hiromasa Iwasaki, for believing in me, inspiring me throughout my career and for writing the Foreword of this book. I am also grateful to my late grandfather Mohammed Hamdi Al-Tamimi for making me the man I am today.

About the Author

Fawzi Mesmar is an award-winning creative director, game designer, leader, author, public speaker, and mentor who has been in the gaming industry for over two decades in a career that spanned the Middle East, New Zealand, Japan, and Europe working for companies such as Ubisoft, Electronics Arts, Activision Blizzard King, Gameloft, and Atlus to name a few.

As a game designer/director, he has worked on more than 20 titles that have been enjoyed by millions of players worldwide, most notably games in the *Mario+Rabbids*, *Star Wars*, *Battlefield*, *Candy Crush*, and *Persona* franchises.

As a manager, he was in line management and leadership positions in different companies with varied cultures around the world, which created a unique blend in management style, overseeing teams of varying sizes.

As an author, he wrote the first ever text book about game design in Arabic: *Al-Khallab on the Art of Game Design* (Kindle Direct Publication, 2018). Fawzi co-authored nine comic books under the Men of Honor series (sold five million copies in MENA). He's a columnist at Pocket Gamer Arabia and blogs frequently about game design and the business of making games.

Fawzi speaks regularly at many global gaming conventions such as GDC, Reboot Develop, Devcom, Gamescom congress, GIC, NZGDC, DWGC, MEGA, MGDC, White Nights, Games Forum, Mobile Games Forum, Quo Vadis, Pocket Gamer, and Casual Connect.

As a mentor, he also frequently holds lectures at game design and development schools such as London University of Fine Arts, Breda University of Applied Sciences in the Netherlands, Auckland Media Design School, NYU, Cologne Design University, Auckland University of Technology, American University in Cairo, Berlin Games Academy, Jordan gaming labs, New Zealand lifeway college and many more. He's currently serving on the board of education at Future Games in Stockholm.

He's also a Google mentor, a jury member at the BAFTAs, IMGA (international mobile games awards) and GDCA (game developers choice awards) and countless other regional award ceremonies around the world. Fawzi also co-founded the IGDA chapter in Berlin, Germany.

Together with fellow Arab game developers Rami Ismail and Osama Dorias, he's part of "The Habibis", a popular podcast about Arab culture, game development, and creativity.

Fawzi was the winner of the Ambassador Award at Game Developers Choice Awards in 2024 and Game Dev Heroes Award in 2020 for the category of Game Design for his contributions to the field. Fawzi was named future class by the Game Awards in 2022 and he was also one of Gamesindustry.biz 100 game changers of the year 2020.

Fawzi holds a Bachelor's degree in Computer Science from the University of Jordan, and a Masters in business administration from Durham University in the UK.

Introduction

I consider myself to be very fortunate and lucky for many things. Perhaps, the thing I'm most lucky for is that I always knew what I wanted to do in life, I knew from an incredibly young age that I wanted to dedicate my life to video games. That made all future life decisions for me fairly simple. I would ask myself the question, "If I do this, would it enable me to make video games?" If the answer was no, then I was not interested. Even if NASA were to call me up to join them, if the job had nothing to do with video games, then I'm just not interested. As I went through life and met many people, I've come to realize how difficult it is to figure out what you want to do, let alone have such a sharp measurement for decision-making. I am grateful for that.

The person to thank for this obsession is my father. He never really worked in information technology as his entire career was in pharmaceutical and medical equipment companies. He did believe, however, that computing was the future; he struggled to figure it out, but that never stopped him from trying to get the latest and the greatest that he could afford and present it to us as his kids. My infatuation with video games started when I was around 3 years old. My dad had just bought an Atari 2600 as a gift for my sister who is 5 years my senior. The console came with three games: Space Invaders, Yar's Revenge, and Hangman. For whatever reason, my sister grew tired of the system rather quickly, leaving it to me most of the time. I was obsessed. I am completely consumed in those imaginary worlds, playing for countless hours and getting lots of other games for the system on my upcoming couple of birthdays. In Jordan, I was one of the few kids in my neighborhood that had one.

In the following year, my father bought himself an IBM 286. It was the first personal computer I've seen; it was a beast of a machine that needed its own desk to hold the tower, a very clicky keyboard, mouse, and an old school TV-sized monitor. The mouse was very peculiar for me, as it was this large plastic cube with three keyboard buttons on top of it and a heavy, dense rubber ball inside of it. None of the software seemed to be using that thing. The hard drive capacity was four full megabytes, and it had a mighty RAM of 16 kilobytes. It ran DOS as an operating system, and my father wanted to generally edit documents and worksheets using a software called Lotus 123 to use for work. He must've quickly grown tired of me as I jumped on his desk and used that machine as soon as he went away to do something else, and often he'd come back from work to find me in his chair editing documents or writing another one of my many novellas and short stories about me and my toys. Most importantly, I have figured out by then how to utilize that large floppy disc drive and that the machine came with multiple games on 8-inch floppy disks, so I was jumping in between messing around with DOS, my dad's work files, my written masterpieces, and playing a lot of Commander Keen and Rambo. While my dad expressed that he was proud of me being able to figure out this machine that completely puzzled him, he still wanted me out of there, and to do that, he got me my very own MSX computer. I was five years old at the time, which was also the year I got into first grade in elementary school. I don't know how my parents pulled it off, but I was one year younger than all of my classmates. I got used to being the youngest of my peers for a long period of my life.

The MSX was the device where I encountered code for the first time. The device itself had two cartridge slots, where you would generally slot in games from a library seemingly entirely owned by Konami at the time, *King's Valley* was my absolute favorite. The machine also came with a cartridge you can write software on, and you can utilize a BASIC compiler that came with the machine. I wrote my first code, and then, the software drew a giant red circle with my name in the middle of it. By then, I knew I wanted to make games, though I had no idea how this circle and video games are generally connected.

When I was in middle school, the first Resident Evil came out on the first PlayStation, and it blew my mind. In 1996 in the Middle East, we didn't have widespread internet just yet, and during those years I used to finish a game, then replay it while writing by hand what I was doing on a school notebook—a walkthrough, basically—and end up helping other kids in class finish that game too. So I was doing a similar walk-through for Resident Evil, tracing the map of the Spencer mansion and highlighting where the key to opening the door was. That was when it hit me. I was tracing what I'm seeing directly and drawing it on my note-book. The moment of insight was that somewhere in Japan, *someone* imagined all of this and made it a reality for me to trace. They came up with this out of nowhere. That insight made me realize what being a game designer meant for the first time, and how it was the job I must have. This was also my first true encounter with how a creative process comes to be, and my endless fascination with creativity in game devel-opment began.

How do people even come up with these ideas?

I started getting my hands on whatever magazine on game develop-ment I could find, reading interviews with these *wizards* that make all these magical worlds I spent my childhood years living in.

It became clear that I needed to learn computers if I ever wanted to make games and probably Japanese because all of my favorite games were made over there. So I studied both. By 16, I had finished high-school and started doing my Bachelor's degree in Computer Science at the University of Jordan in Amman. With a group of friends, we also approached the Embassy of Japan, who organized classes for us to learn the language. In one of those classes, I met a crew of like-minded peeps who also dreamed about making a video game.

By 2003, a group of eight of us, from different walks of life but mostly computer science students, few about to graduate, decided to make a game on the Nintendo Gameboy Advance (GBA) console. A few of our members can use that project as their university thesis graduation proj-ect as well. We called ourselves Team Elements. At first, we used to gather all day in a corner booth at a Burger King. The eight of us shared a few coke glasses that we were refilling all day as we were putting our ideas about what the project is together.

Soon, we outstayed our welcome at the Burger King, and we ended up renting a very small space above a baker store in the neighborhood where most of us lived. We brought our own computers from home and some plastic chairs and tables that one of us had in their backyard. The space was small enough that we could only fit four computers in and had to work in shifts. The bakers furnace was directly underneath us, which meant it was very hot in there, in an already very hot country, mind you. But we didn't care, as we always had fresh bread to eat around "the office."

We worked on two projects simultaneously, one of them was code named "Phantoms", a side-scrolling slasher where you play as a shinobi called Okami (Japanese for Wolf), and project "A-RPG" a chrono triggered inspired turn-based role-playing game that took part in Petra and was completely playable in Arabic, though the GBA did not have native Arabic language support. My role on both projects was to write the music, I had a band back then, and I played gigs all over the country. Given that both games were 2 MB each and my budget for the music and sound effects was under 200 KB, I needed to be creative and work from those constraints. I used code to layer in and play the music I wrote, utilizing close to 40 instruments. The guys on my team liked the design decisions I was contributing with and probably hated the code I was writing, so they eventually opted to have me be the game designer of the games in addition to my work on music. I have been a game designer ever since, though it was under different titles and levels of seniority. I still think game designer is the job title that describes me best.

We ended up finishing an entire vertical slice of both projects running on GBA hardware that we hacked as we had no access to official dev kits. The Middle East wasn't even on the distribution channels for games back then, and companies couldn't imagine that there were people playing games in that region, let alone wanting to make them. We presented the demos to a jury of professors in my teammates' graduation defense. They were completely confused by what they were looking at. Waving the GBA around, they lectured us on how we should've done something more useful with our skills, like making a website or an HR system. My teammates received a D+ grade for the project, barely passing the graduation mark, and they sent us packing.

Pretty soon afterwards, our leader Mohammed Khashashneh received an offer to work in a software company in Japan, and by pursuing it he was realizing his dream. Other peeps followed suit getting "real jobs" and our team was no more.

George Shomali, a local gaming enthusiast, had just returned to the country after successfully selling his company in Saudi Arabia and wanting to make a game for PC and console. As we were few of the people to have even attempted to make a game in the region, he hired all of us and hired a team to train around us. We ended up being close to 50 people at Nassons Entertainment Studios, with myself, the head creative/design guy, overseeing the projects at the age of 23. It was during my time there that I got to travel to Japan for the first time and actually get to pitch our game to publishers in Tokyo. One of which was Nintendo. The discussion I had with the reps at the time is something that stayed with me. The guy told me that the world has gotten used to seeing games coming in from Japanese or Western developers, who have managed to translate their experiences and cultures to the world. Players around the world got to experience what it's like to be a samurai or a Shinobi or a cowboy or a medieval knight through the games that came out of established studios. "But games about your culture and your part of the world is something that we have never seen before" he told me, "You have the responsibility to make games that exports your identity to the world."

We can't create what we don't know. Everything we make will, without a doubt, come from somewhere in our life experience. Cultural backgrounds and ideologies are the ones that are most instinctive to us, which is why it's so evident in our creations—gaming or otherwise—and it's a notion I focus on quite significantly in this book.

Since my early days in Jordan, my career has taken me around the world, from working as a designer for Atlus on Persona, to a principal designer on IP tie-in games at Gameloft in New Zealand, to a creative director on local market only vita games in Japan, to leading design and production for *Candy Crush* in Germany, to heading up design for Battlefield at EA DICE in Sweden, to overseeing creative on several projects in different European studios at Ubisoft like *Mario+Rabbids Sparks of Hope* or *Star Wars Outlaws*. Regardless of where I was in the world, I was always teaching game design, from Auckland University of science and technology, Berlin Games Academy, Cologne Design University, London University of Arts, NYU, to Future Games in Stockholm where I hold a position on the board of education for the school.

I have worked with hundreds of designers, students, and indie developers throughout my journey as well as dozens of creative directors and leaders. I had a lot of observations about how those peeps came up with ideas, their understanding of their creative voice, and how they spoke about it. I often mused that I was in the *idea business* due to the nature of my day job and my education passion. I was in a situation where lots of different people were pitching and discussing their ideas with me. I started to see patterns about how people come up with ideas, how people react when their ideas are discussed, and how others struggle to be able to articulate their ideas and get others behind them.

The topic of creativity and innovation is something that comes up in my line of work on a daily basis, it's critical to my industry and to the success of the games we make. It's also a heavily debated topic with many different and conflicting opinions on the matter.

I wanted to write this book to put together several factors. The observations that I have had working with so many highly creative individuals, observations I had working with those who think they are highly creative individuals, seeing the different creative processes of people in different parts of the world, my personal creative process, my research and reading into the neuroscience and psychology of creativity, but most importantly, the significant contribution mindfulness and reflection make to the creative process as whole.

I start this book by coming to an agreement with a reader on a definition of creativity that we will use for the remainder of this book. That creativity goes beyond simply creating things. Then I try to support that by diving deeper to illustrate how inspiration works. How do we get inspired? What inspires us, and what acts as a source of inspiration? Those two chapters equip the reader with a holistic view of what ideas are and how they are formed, preparing them for the main message that I'm advocating for in my work.

If you are to take one thing from what I'm presenting to you here, I would urge you to reflect and consider the concept of creative sobriety in Chapter 3. Creative sobriety is a term I'm coining, and it's your ability to differentiate between a concept and how that concept has touched you, then achieving originality by an act of creation guided by that impression. It's about reflecting on all the events in your life journey that had led you to this moment of the spark of the idea and then intellectually determining with courage that is needed to move forward and bring something new to the world.

My method in teaching is always to arm my students with the theory, then pose questions for them to reflect on, so that they will view their own problems armed with that knowledge. I wouldn't want to give the reader or student a step-by-step guide on how to handle a situation because every person and situation are different and have so much complexity that no framework or method will ever catch all. What I aim to do is to help introduce a way of thinking and considering things and hope that your interpretation of it will help you to find those solutions and, in the best case, your own creative voice.

However, I know that many who will get their hands on this book will want more practical methodologies to take away from reading this text. In Chapters 4 and 5, I presented several frameworks and methods that are used to both ideate and to determine value once those ideas are generated. We will go in depth into how innovation can work within organizations and teams, how companies can foster a creative mindset, and how you can effectively generate as many ideas within a context as possible.

In the final chapter, I offer my opinion on our responsibilities as creatives, toward ourselves, our teams, our industries, and to the world around us. Our ability to manifest ideas and understand them is fundamentally what makes us human. Our ability to be creative is what's caused us to evolve as a species. We all have a role to play; every journey counts, and it's important for us to be aware and considerate of that responsibility.

I hope that wherever you are in your creative journey, you find something in this book that helps you find or reinforce your creative voice. I hope that if you were ever in doubt, some passage here will give you courage. I hope that at the very least, something here will make you wonder, disagree, inspire, challenge, or support you on your creative journey. I would consider this thing a huge success if one person somewhere out there took something from it and it helped them find that gratitude about their mission in life like I have.

I can't wait to experience what you're gifting to the world.

Fawzi Mesmar
Stockholm, Sweden,
June 2024

Chapter 1
Defining creativity

There is no doubt that creativity is the most important human resource of all. Without creativity, there would be no progress, and we would be forever repeating the same patterns.

– Edward De Bono

Before we venture into the depths of the creative process, we may benefit from establishing a common ground to start from a basic definition of the very term we will be deconstructing in order to examine the parts. Let us begin with an attempt to pin down a basic definition of creativity in order to have a solid base to build upon. I've often witnessed great debates around various forms of artistic or cultural production, books and films, games and narratives, over what constitutes a 'creative' work and what makes one worthy of that label. The varying—and often polarized—nature of this debate indicates the breadth of its content and the subjectivity of its definition.

Ideas

At the heart of creativity is the ability to generate ideas and then act upon them. The word itself describes one's ability to manifest something out of nothing. Creativity is so closely associated with ideas, as they are the nucleus from which creation stems. Throughout history, philosophers and intellectuals puzzled over what ideas are and how they appear to us. Idea even comes from the Greek word "idein"

DOI: 10.1201/9781003261834-1

(ἰδέα) which means to see. The ancient Greek philosophers pondered the notion of ideas heavily.

Plato's definition of ideas is also known as the theory of forms; he defined ideas as abstract, eternal, and immutable entities that exist independently of the physical world that we perceive through our senses. Plato viewed ideas as "true reality," as the physical world is a flawed reflection or imitation of those perfect and unchanging forms. For example, the idea of a "circle" represents a perfect and unchanging form of a circle irrespective of any particular instance of a circle we encounter in the real world. Think of ideas as being high-level concepts that we relate everything we detect with our senses.

Those concepts exist outside of time and space; they are of a higher form existing in a plane of existence of their own beyond our material and lower ones. Ideas that exist in that realm are held in higher regard in Plato's eyes than those in the physical ones. For example, the aforementioned "circle" idea is superior to the circular objects we find in our world. To him, a higher concept of "Beauty" is more elevated than various beautiful objects we encounter in our lives—it's as if what we sense is striving to become closer to that perfect concept that exists in abstraction.

In his book *The Republic*, Plato illustrated that through the allegory of the cave, where prisoners trapped in it can only see shadows on the walls cast by the objects that are outside of the cave, the shadows represent the physical world while the objects that cast those shadows represent the world of ideas (Figure 1.1).

He believed that true knowledge could not be gained through the senses of the physical world; instead, knowledge comes from a direct apprehension of the world of ideas through reason and intellectual contemplation. In Plato's definition, creativity is the manifestation of ideas. They are the ultimate reality and the foundation of knowledge that our world is built upon.

Creativity in the brain

If creativity is the manifestation of ideas into actuality, then creativity is not merely making things. It's not any act of creation; it is the act of creation based on how we *perceive* the idea or concept. It is what we make based on our *understanding* of ideas.

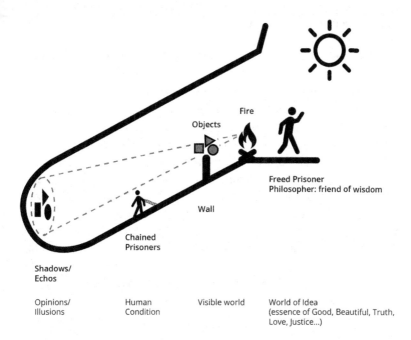

Figure 1.1 Plato's theory of forms.

Creativity, therefore, is very closely related to expression—the ability to translate experience or feelings through a medium that can then be further experienced with others. Paul Cézanne, French impressionist and painter, once said that he aimed "to make visible how the world touches us." To him, there was a clear distinction between making visible how the world was and how the world makes an impression; he viewed creativity as a way to translate how he felt about the world around him for all to see.

A lot of our modern day establishments make things en masse, from factories, to construction companies to accounting firms. Rarely would they be described as creative places to work, though their output is "making" a lot of things. It is worth noting, however, that there are ways perhaps to be creative within a mass production factory if one devises a method to speed up production, revolutionize the amount of effort needed, or greatly reduce pollution. Creativity is hence associated with problem solving just as much as it is with expression. Creativity is a predictor of achievement in the arts just as intellect describes the same in sciences. In fact, from the perspective of how our brains work, there's no difference at all. Dr. Nancy Andreasen (2006), researcher and author of *The Creative Brain*, found that "differences in artistic vs scientific creativity are rare" from a neuroscientific perspective. Her research centered on an assertion against the age-old belief that a single "creative center" exists in the brain. Instead, she elucidates that creativity emerges from a constellation of brain regions working in unison. It's akin to an orchestra, where each instrument contributes uniquely, and it's their collective symphony that brings forth creative thought.

A special section of that orchestra of constellations in the human brain is the default mode network (DMN) when it comes to its contribution to creativity. Activated during seemingly passive activities like daydreaming or introspection, the DMN is the "mind-wandering" network. Moments of introspection or daydreaming, often dismissed as non-productive, are, in fact, the fertile grounds from which creative ideas sprout. The DMN, in these moments, creates a cascade of spontaneous connections, linking seemingly unrelated thoughts, memories, and experiences. Our ability to form novel associations is at the very heart of creative endeavors, from penning a poem to formulating a groundbreaking scientific theory.

Our mind's ability to branch out, to visualize myriad possibilities beyond the obvious, creating an associative connection between several concepts that are at face value seemingly disconnected is called *divergent thinking*. Dr. Andreasen highlights the specific brain areas that light up when individuals engage in tasks that require divergent thinking. These regions, associated with attention, cognitive control, and working memory, are evidence that creative thought is a rigorous mental exercise, demanding an intricate dance of neural activities.

An important participant in that dance is also the Central Executive Network (CEN), which is crucial for planning and decision-making. It's the filter or inhibitor—the network that helps us make decisions about what ideas we pursue. It might help an artist determine the composition of a painting or a writer the general structure that they want to follow as they're putting their book together.

It is interesting to note that creative activities that require more absent thinking than inhibition, such as musical improvisation, activate the DMN much more than the CEN. It was noticed in several studies how the DMN of a freestyle rapper will fire up as they rhyme while the

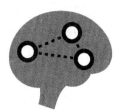  

Default Mode Network

Activates when not performing a
task; daydreaming, mind-
wandering, thinking about others

Salience Network

Switching between
the Default Mode Network and
the Central Executive Network

Central Executive Network

Engages your conscious brain
to think and maintains
attention on a prioritized task

Figure 1.2 Different networks of the brain.

CEN will be a lot less engaged as if the rate of output requires much less filtering on the spot (Figure 1.2).

It's worth noting that the inner working of the brain is very complex; the network's illustrations are simplified to deliver a message. Dr. Andreasen's insights into these networks underscore the holistic nature of creativity. It's not just about the "Eureka" moment when the connection is made and the idea is born but also about refining, evaluating, and executing the idea, all of which require a seamless integration of multiple brain systems. We will venture into the methods in which we cultivate and stimulate ideations for those Eureka moments to happen in the creative process chapter of this book (Chapter 5).

Creativity in Arts, Sciences, and Beyond

Divergent thinking is not confined to traditionally "creative" professions. A scientist pondering multiple hypotheses or a business professional brainstorming solutions utilizes the same neural pathways. This universality implies that we all possess the inherent neural machinery for creativity, although its manifestation might differ based on individual experiences and environments.

Like Paul Cézanne, artists have long used their canvases as vehicles of expression, conveying beyond visual representations. Techniques, color choice, composition, and approach embody a piece that is the artist's own perspective, which in turn evokes a visceral response in the viewer. A great example of this is impressionism, a revolutionary art movement that emerged in the late 19th century that wanted to depart from traditional approaches to painting, generating an impact that continues to be celebrated till this day.

Cézanne was part of a small group of young painters who gathered in private workshops with the objective of creating something different. That group included many greats in French art history, like Edouard Manet, Edgar Degas, Auguste Renoir, Camille Pissaro, and Claude Monet. When Manet's "Luncheon on the Grass" painting was refused from the Salon de Paris exhibition for straying too far from what was considered artistic standards of the time, the group organized the "Salon des Refusés" or Exhibition of the Refused, to showcase their work. This is where Claude Monet presented his "Impression, Sunrise" becoming a target of critics calling the exhibition "L'éxposition des impression-nistes" (The Impressionist Exhibition) to denounce the unfinished aspect of the works. The critics unknowingly gave the name to one of the most successful movements in modern art history (Figure 1.3).

Figure 1.3 "Impression, Sunrise" (1872), Claude Monet, Musée Marmottan Monet, Paris.

Monet painted "Impression, Sunrise" depicting the harbor of Le Havre, his hometown. It portrays the early morning sun with several boats on the water and their reflection on the water rendered with quick strokes. The scene itself is shrouded in a mist, which in turn blends the sea with the sky, creating an atmosphere instead of a detailed painting. At the time of the painting's creation in 1872, Monet was focused on painting directly while in nature, often working very quickly to capture the essence of the landscape within a moment in time with a focus on light and mood. He utilized rapid brushstrokes and a vivid color palette to capture the fleeting effects of light. He had a disregard for detail, and to many in the era, his work appeared as if were unfinished. This approach was a significant departure from the detailed, polished style of academic painting. Critics were accustomed to the detailed, finished quality of traditional painting and found Monet's style to be crude, though the critics soon began to appreciate the unique beauty and innovative qualities of this and other impressionist paintings.

Impressionism had a profound impact on the art world, including paving the way for various modern art movements. The emphasis on light, color, and everyday subject matter influenced post-impressionists like Vincent van Gogh to create many masterpieces. The movement played a crucial role in the transition from traditional to modern art, flipping the script entirely on the rigid conventions of art of its time. Most importantly, however, it encouraged artists to view the world in a different way entirely. Monet once said, "When you go out to paint, try to forget what objects you have before you, a tree, a house, a field, or whatever. Merely think, here is a little square of blue, here an oblong of pink, here a streak of yellow." Monet encouraged the artist to relay their perception and experience in their art rather than visually render what is there as is. Monet and impressionists often painted everyday life and scenes from the modern world, including urban landscapes, leisure activities, and people in natural settings. However, the final outcome was always a deeply personal representation of all of us and what the artist perceived and experienced. Creativity for Monet wasn't the body of work, but the range of expression.

Cézanne afterwards is acclaimed for laying the groundwork for the transition from 19th-century conceptions of artistic endeavor to a new, radically different world of art in the 20th century. His approach to brushwork was distinctive. He built up color in layers, using thick, coalescing brushstrokes that created a tactile sense of the substance. This method was a departure from the more fluid and fleeting brushstrokes of the Impressionists. His unique eye however, morphed reality into his own vision, Cézanne often played with perspective, flattening the space and emphasizing the two-dimensionality of the canvas. He was known for exploring geometric forms in his compositions, simplifying natural forms into cylinders, spheres, and cones.

One of his most celebrated works is "The Mont Sainte-Victoire" series. These paintings depict the Sainte-Victoire mountain in Provence, France, and are renowned for their portrayal of color, light, and geometric form. Cézanne was deeply attached to his native Provence, and this connection profoundly influenced his art. Mont Sainte-Victoire, a mountain that dominated the landscape near his home, became an obsessive subject for him. He painted it numerous times, in various lights, seasons, and from different viewpoints. In these paintings, Cézanne not only captured the essence of the Provençal landscape but also experimented with form, color, and composition.

Cézanne's work constitutes a bridge between late 19th-century impressionism and the early 20th century's new line of artistic inquiry, Cubism. Picasso is said to have remarked that Cézanne "is the father of us all." His reduction of natural forms to their geometric essentials laid the foundation for modern abstraction. Though his work initially was a continuation of the impressionist movement, Cézanne's creativity was in generating ideas that were deep in his personal experiences, the art he studied, his group of Refuses, his hometown, and like many of his era, the desire for art to move away from classic customs of art and realism in paintings, as that was rendered almost pointless with the invention of the photographic cameras. These elements and countless others, propelled Cézanne and Monet to focus on expression instead of pure technique, to render the world as they saw it, not to simply recreate it as a camera would.

Similar to the artists turning to creativity to go against classic art norms, many scientific discoveries and breakthroughs have occurred when scientists questioned prevailing theories and what was considered common knowledge, utilizing keen observations as they were exploring uncharted territories. Sometimes quite literally.

In 1831, at the age of 22, Charles Darwin embarked on a journey on the HMS Beagle as a naturalist. The voyage was intended to map the coast of South America, but it provided Darwin with a unique opportunity to study geology, botany, and zoology across various parts of the globe. During the voyage, Darwin observed a wide array of geological formations, fossils, and living organisms. He collected numerous specimens—from insects to birds, to plants and fossils—meticulously noting details about their characteristics and the environments in which they were found.

When the Beagle reached the Galápagos Islands Darwin observed finches with a variety of beak shapes. He noted that the beak shape varied from island to island and seemed to be adapted to different types of food sources. He began to realize that species might change over time and adapt to their environments. This was a significant shift from the prevailing view of the time, which largely held that species were unchanging.

After returning to England, Darwin spent decades analyzing his collections and expanding on his ideas through research and correspondence with other naturalists. He was influenced by the work of other scientists and thinkers. Notably, Thomas Malthus's essay on populations suggested that struggle and competition were fundamental aspects of existence, which contributed to Darwin's understanding of natural selection. By the 1840s, Darwin had formulated his theory but hesitated to publish it due to its controversial nature. It wasn't until Alfred Russel Wallace, another naturalist, independently came up with a similar theory that Darwin was compelled to present his findings.

Darwin and Wallace jointly presented papers on natural selection to the Linnean Society of London. This was followed by the publication of *On the Origin of Species* in 1859, where Darwin laid out his theory in detail. The book was both controversial and highly influential, altering scientific thought about biological diversity and the processes that drive the emergence of new species as we know them.

In remarkable similarity, Darwin's personal experience and life journey were a direct link to his scientific discoveries; his travels exposed him to observe the world through a lens few people of his time had, divergent thinking, combined with his natural sense of curiosity and courage to challenge the norm of scientific circles of the time to present a theory that changed our very understanding of ourselves as a species as well as all living things on Earth.

There are domains that combine both artistic and scientific ingenuity, such as fields of architecture, industrial design, or even application development. Architects need to be armed with the science of what is needed for a structure to carry its own weight, stand the deterioration caused by time and weather elements, and resist natural forces such as wind and in some territories of the world even earthquakes. Architects need to be aware of the regulations that need to be followed in a certain state, the ventilation needed to create a suitable climate for people to dwell within those structures and many more scientific and regulatory requirements. Yet, they are able to bend all of these requirements with their own understanding and expression of space and meaning, capable of creating structures that are capable of allowing them to feel a certain thing.

Daniel Libeskind is a Polish-American architect who has won many awards for his renowned career having designed several iconic buildings around the globe. Among the ones he's most known for his first project: an extension to the historic Jewish museum in Berlin. Libeskind's parents were Polish jews and holocaust survivors, adding a lot to his familiarity and informing his design. His approach in designing the structure is highly experiential and narrative-driven, dubbed "Between the Line." Much of the zigzaggy titanium clad building is deliberately designed to have the visitor go through a series of emotions enthralled by the building itself, not just the exhibits. With no entrances and exits of its own, the visitor can only access the extension through an underground tunnel symbolizing how hidden the Jewish history is. Several concrete voids cut through the building, with one holding an installation artwork by Menashe Kadishman featuring over 10,000 metal faces in a screaming expression that the visitor walks on and symbolizes humanity reduced to ash.

"It's an experience, and some of it is foreboding," said Libeskind. "Some of it is inspiring, some of it is full of light. Some of it is dark, some of it is disorienting, and some of it is orienting. That was my intent in creating a building that tells a story, not just an abstract set of walls and windows" Astbury (2022).

In many ways, the words of Cézanne ring true in this example, where Cézanne wanted to make visible how the world touches us,

Libeskind wanted to make traversable how a specific part of our world and history touches us. His knowledge of the psychology of space created feelings in people as they walked through the hallways he designed.

Game design, similar to architecture, is another one of those fields that combine scientific domains of knowledge and artistic ingenuity. Designers need to be aware of the technology limitations that are being used and wield them to create video games that speak to us when we play them and put us in the driver's seat of the main protagonist, allowing us to feel what's it like to be in the shoes of someone else in a manner very few other mediums can.

Papers, Please won one award after the other after it came out in 2013. The game puts the player in the shoes of a passport control officer at the border of a fictional dystopian country called Arstotzka. The player must check immigrants' documentation against an ever-growing list of requirements under the pressure of time, moral dilemmas, and consequences of actions, allowing the player to decide who can enter or who must be turned away or even detained.

"At some point I'd done enough international traveling to start noticing the rigamarole that immigration inspectors do when checking your documents," said sole developer Lucas Pope in a gamedeveloper.com interview (Alexander, 2023). "I thought that whatever correlations they were doing could be turned into some fun game mechanics." Having spent long years working professionally as a game developer for major studios, including Naughty Dog, Pope already had a very good grasp of the technical know-how that is needed to build games and the experience to identify the scope of an experience that he could develop on his own. He also wanted to explore unique, personal, and interesting game ideas that are outside of the usual themes of commercial game releases. He lifted inspiration directly from his personal experience and personal observation. He wanted to make playable how the world touches us and affects people that you normally wouldn't meet.

"The game concept focuses on approaching things in a different direction than usual, so a big part of the design was taking commonly-seen events and turning them around to put you on the other side," explained Pope. He goes on to say, "In the end though, I really didn't need to say much about the world; the player's imagination handles most of the heavy lifting."

Originality

Creativity is not to recreate. For someone to write the tyger down on a notepad after it has already been written by William Blake will not be described as creativity, nor is following the instructions of a Lego set to build the model on the box, nor will they follow a step-by-step video tutorial on how to paint the Mona Lisa exactly the same way Da Vinci did (if such a video even exists). It's that exact need to not recreate is what pushed Cézanne, Monet, and other artists to render images a camera can't capture and mass produce.

This means that novelty is an integral part of what is dubbed creative. One would often hear the words creative being synonymous or paired with others, such as fresh, new, or never seen before. Even uniqueness doesn't seem to give the word justice because a recreation of a fargone historic monument however will forever be labeled a replica even if only one of them exists in the world.

Novelty comes with the heavy load of the creation, which is completely and utterly unprecedented. To be an origin of inspiration for future creations that will come after it, this is where the term originality even comes from.

To be original is to come up with something that surprises us. Surprise in this notion is not necessarily shocking. It is to come up with the unexpected, something that is understood within the context yet not familiar enough to cause us to stop and think. Originality then, is when an idea is statistically infrequent or rare.

In stand-up comedy, the element of surprise often determines the success or failure of a performance. Comedians even artificially manufacture surprise through subversion. They would craft scenarios that encourage audiences to predict outcomes, only to then swiftly pivot in unforeseen directions. This intentional disruption of expectations makes us laugh. By shifting the narrative suddenly, comedians not only elicit immediate reactions but also engrain the comedic moment in the minds of their audience. A joke remembered, after all, is a joke well-told.

Moreover, surprise in comedy has the power to stimulate thought. By juxtaposing the familiar with the unexpected, comedians offer fresh perspectives on everyday situations, societal norms, or even deep-seated prejudices. This not only amplifies the humor but also encourages audiences to engage critically with their preconceived notions. The term "punch line" refers to the shocking diversion at the end of a joke, resembling the shock of a punch to the face. Jokes surprise us and therefore delight us. Ones that we "see coming" simply do not.

Originality is to identify what the norms or expectations are and then cleverly avoid them, presenting them in an unforeseen manner that we don't see coming. It's what you would call "flipping the script."

There's been lots of discussion about the importance of surprise in creating moments that have a long-lasting effect. In their book *Power of Moments: Why Certain Experiences Have Extraordinary Impact* (2017), Chip Heath and Dan Heath delve into the anatomy of moments that have a profound impact on individuals. At its core, the book posits that while life may be a series of experiences, only a few truly stick out and shape us, and there's an art and science to creating such defining moments.

One of the pivotal elements in crafting these impactful moments is the element of surprise. According to the Heath brothers, surprise acts as a powerful catalyst, intensifying our emotions and etching experiences deeper into our memories. This is because unexpected events or stimuli grab our attention more effectively, forcing our brains to focus and process the novelty of the situation.

One establishment that does that really well is a small hotel in Los Angeles. The Magic Castle Hotel is unique, and its distinctiveness arises not necessarily from opulent luxury or architectural grandeur, but from its exceptional dedication to guest experience through standout offerings. It has chosen to redefine luxury, not in terms of tangible opulence, but in the richness of experiences and the delight of the unexpected.

Take, for instance, the now-legendary Popsicle Hotline. On an unassuming cherry-red phone stationed by the pool, once the guest lifts the receiver, a white-gloved staff member delivers a complimentary popsicle in the flavor of their choice. This surprise, far removed from the conventional extravagances one might expect, creates a magical experience in the minds of its guests. Speaking of magic, all the waiters at the hotel can perform magic tricks, and they will frequently perform as they're taking orders or clearing the breakfast plates. For anyone who's staying for a weekend in LA, any one of the hotel's many surprises is sure to leave a lasting effect and a story for them to tell once they go home.

We don't have to wait for these moments to happen; instead, we can intentionally engineer them. By integrating surprise, we can elevate experiences, turning ordinary situations into memorable, standout events. This isn't about grand gestures, but rather infusing elements of unexpected delight, recognition, or insight into daily scenarios.

By carefully considering surprise as part of creation, it inevitably moves the creator closer toward originality. A lot of video game creators are also known for their heavy use of flipping the script and surprising the players in ways they never saw coming.

Legendary creative director Hideo Kojima is recognized for his signature approach to crafting game narratives and mechanics. His design philosophy often incorporates unexpected elements, aiming to provide players with experiences that diverge from the norm.

The *Metal Gear Solid* series is filled with examples of Kojima's use of surprise. His design often toys with meta aspects of gaming where he blurs the lines of the fourth wall, subtly involving players in the narrative and prompting them to reflect on their role within the game's universe. One of the most famous examples of this is the inventive battle with Psycho Mantis, a boss enemy that possesses psychic abilities and is therefore able to dodge all of the player's attacks because he can "read" them before they land. The battle required players to adapt by switching their controller ports, confusing the Mantis and allowing the player to defeat him. Another example from the PlayStation One classic was the moment the player was to call another character in the game. For them to find the frequency, they had to look at one of the screenshots at the back of the game disc.

In *Metal Gear Solid 2: Sons of Liberty*, players spend a significant portion of the game not as the expected protagonist, Solid Snake, but as the new character Raiden. This was not just a surprise for the sake of it, but a deep commentary on the nature of sequels, expectations, and player agency. Kojima went as far as altering some game footage for promotional material to show Snake in sections he won't reach in the final product to further support the narrative in the player's mind that they will play the same protagonist in the much anticipated sequel.

The surprise in those designs serves as more than just an unexpected twist. It's an avenue to enhance emotional engagement, creating moments that provoke thought and discussion among players.

Kojima's surprises are intertwined with themes and messages he wishes to convey, leaving a long lasting impact on players and cementing his place in player's hearts as one of the most celebrated game creators of our time.

Value

We've established how novelty or surprise are connected to originality, in fact it is what renders an idea to be unique or unusual compared to other ideas within the same plane at any given time.

The value of an idea comes from the appropriateness, relevance, or fit of that idea. In other words, it is how suitable and meaningful that idea is to a certain context. The idea will inevitably solve a problem—including self-enforced ones such as creative vision, which we will discuss later—or is a suitable response to a given situation or aids in accomplishing a certain goal.

A solar-powered flashlight is a novel idea, but its practicality is questionable since it would be most needed in the dark when it can't recharge. Waterproof tea bags is another example since teabags are meant to be immersed in water. Making them waterproof while novel, would negate their primary function. A movement advocating for abandoning all reading in order to "free the mind": While surprising, it undermines centuries of knowledge and the benefits of literacy.

Determining the value of an idea is only done within a defined context. Therefore oftentimes in order for creativity to be truly unleashed, a very clear context must be established. That is usually in the form of the constraints or boundaries within which we should create the desired outcome that we want to arrive at.

In the example of the waterproof tea bags that was stated earlier, if the context is to create something useful, then that idea has no value, but in the context of challenging, the very notion of what tea bags even are and what they're used for, then waterproof tea bags can be considered quite creative and original.

Determining value therefore is worth stopping at, as it is nuanced and can be interpreted in various ways depending on the context. It can normally fall into one of the following buckets:

- **Functional Value:** An idea or artifact can be considered creative if it has practical utility or solves a particular problem. For instance, the invention of the wheel was not only new and surprising in its time but also immensely valuable in terms of its functionality, revolutionizing transportation and machinery.
- **Aesthetic Value:** In art and design, value might be gauged in terms of aesthetic 'appeal or emotional impact. For example, Vincent van Gogh's "Starry Night" is not only a novel representation of the night sky but is also valued for its beauty, use of color, and the emotional depth it conveys.
- **Intellectual Value:** In academic and philosophical contexts, value can be measured by the depth of insight or understanding an idea offers. Einstein's theory of relativity, for instance, was not just a new approach to understanding the physical world, but it also held immense intellectual value, reshaping centuries of thought in physics.
- **Social and Cultural Value:** Ideas or movements that bring about social change or influence cultural paradigms can be seen as valuable. The writings of Martin Luther King Jr., which played a significant role in advancing the civil rights movement, were not only new and surprising in their time but also held profound social value.
- **Moral Value:** Sometimes, creativity might be gauged by the ethical or moral significance of an idea. For example, Mahatma Gandhi's approach to non-violent resistance was a novel strategy in the political struggles of his time, and its value lay in its moral stance against oppression and violence.

Value comes from a context in which we generate original ideas; it is also one of the lenses through which we determine if an idea is worth pursuing. It provides appropriateness to the subject matter we're trying to express ourselves through.

Creativity within Constraints

While the concept of creativity often evokes images of unbridled freedom and endless possibilities, the reality is that constraints, paradoxically, play a crucial role in fostering deeper, more nuanced creativity.

It's essential to recognize that constraints are an inherent part of our existence. From the laws of physics that govern our universe to the societal norms that guide our behaviors, boundaries are ever omnipresent. Even when we consider our jobs, constraints can be seen in the form of budget limitations, technological challenges, cultural contexts, or specific client needs. And while it might seem counterintuitive, limitations are catalysts for profound creative breakthroughs. Constraints compel designers and creators to think more deeply and critically about their work. When faced with a limitation, the direct path to a solution is often blocked, necessitating the need to explore alternative routes. The haiku, a traditional form of Japanese poetry, requires adherence to a strict 5–7–5 syllabic pattern. That might sound very limiting, but some of the most evocative and profound verses in literature are haikus. Poets were forced to distill their sentiments into that concise, yet impactful format, with centuries of creativity in that format to prove it.

Constraints can bring clarity. The sheer range of options when thinking unbounded, endless possibilities can be paralyzing. It's the paradox of choice, where an abundance of options can lead to anxiety and indecision. Constraints narrow the scope for us, making the creative process more manageable. Short films require storytellers to convey a narrative within a limited timeframe. Directors of those movies have to use every second, prompting them to hone in on the essential elements of their story, leading to sharp, compelling narratives.

Design within constraints often engenders a deeper connection with the target audience. When creators understand and design within the specific constraints of their audience's needs or the contexts in which their creations will be used, the end product often resonates more deeply. IKEA, the Swedish furniture giant, designs keeping in mind the constraints of flat-pack shipping and self-assembly, greatly reducing costs and space storage needed for both the company and the customer, resulting in products that are both functional and contextually relevant.

Silent Hill is a survival horror game developed by Konami and released in 1999 for the original PlayStation. The game was universally acclaimed when it came out, as critics and players alike were captivated by the game's focus on atmosphere and creative vision, which wanted to push the boundaries in horror games by focusing less on jump scares and more on building tension on the psychological aspect of horror. One of the most iconic features that defined the atmosphere of the game was that the titular town was shrouded by a thick layer of fog. This fog, however, was not only there to build tension, as it was a direct response to the PlayStation's technical constraints.

The PlayStation, groundbreaking as it was, had limitations in rendering detailed 3D environments. There could only be so many objects rendered on screen before the polycount (number of polygons on screen) or the amount of textures stored in the memory proved to be too much for the hardware. When those values are exceeded, the game will slow down to the point that makes it unplayable. Game developers would normally resort to limiting the number of characters and objects displayed on screen at the same time or create characters that had a very low poly count (which might explain why a lot of games of that era had low detailed characters). Another metric developerscan use is the draw distance or how far ahead objects in the game world are displayed in detail; the shorter it is, the fewer objects need to be visible. So for *Silent Hill* to have the graphical quality that the team needed, the draw distance was relatively short due to these constraints. For games with vast areas or open-world environments, this could lead to a disruptive phenomenon where objects would pop into view abruptly, breaking the immersive experience for players.

To address this, the team behind *Silent Hill* implemented the thick fog that consistently blankets the town. This reduced the player's visible draw distance, ensuring that the game only displayed what was immediately surrounding the player. This method ensured a smooth transition between the unrendered outskirts and the detailed immediate environment, making objects slowly materialize from the fog rather than suddenly appear, offering a more fluid visual experience. But beyond its technical utility, the fog played an immense role in the game's atmospheric design. It created a palpable sense of vulnerability, uncertainty, and isolation. The fog meant that threats would remain hidden until they were dangerously close, making every step in *Silent Hill* fraught with tension. Additionally, the fog complemented the narrative's themes, symbolizing the unclear memories of the protagonist and the town's own murky mysteries.

Furthermore, the fog's presence transformed the auditory experience of the game. With reduced visibility, players found themselves more dependent on the game's sound cues. While most survival horror games focused on darkness to hide enemies and build atmosphere, *Silent Hill* was able to achieve a similar feeling even in broad daylight. The faint and distant echoes of footsteps, unsettling ambient noises, or even the static from the main character's radio, which signaled an approaching enemy, became central to the gameplay experience. The soundscape of *Silent Hill* was enhanced by the fog, as threats would often be audible long before they were visible, creating a suspenseful dynamic.

The innovative use of fog in *Silent Hill* showcases the immense creative potential that can arise from technical limitations. Instead of being merely a workaround, the fog became central to the game's identity, highlighting that often in design, challenges can lead to the most memorable solutions. The creators of *Silent Hill* not only found a valuable solution to their problem, but they managed to package it in a way that surprised players and challenged the norms of the genre of the time. Launching a franchise of games that continue to this day and a legacy of games—and movies—that are often referenced whenever new horror games are made.

Creative Vision

There are times in which constraints come from within, where self-imposed constraints shape, guide, and provide depth to one's work. That is often referred to as creative vision; it is an intricate interplay between context and constraint that offers profound insights into the essence of artistry and creation. It's when thinking of blue sky and trying to create boundaries with it that are based on personal preferences and purpose. It's creating the context to which originality can become appropriate.

Creative vision is the measurement that all creators can use to judge if an idea is valuable or not in the context they are creating in. It can be likened to an artist's compass, guiding their journey through the vast landscape of possibility. It's an intrinsic blueprint, detailing not just what is to be created but, more importantly, how it's to be approached. At its core, this vision sets parameters, acting as both a guiding star and a boundary marker. When identified correctly, creators can use it for themselves to judge the decisions they're making, and when communicated broadly, the team of creators that are working on the project will be able to judge if the part they're contributing to is servicing the vision of the final outcome.

Many people recognize Wes Anderson as a visionary filmmaker of motion pictures. His films are almost instantly identifiable because of their unique aesthetics, narrative cadence, and attention to detail. Rich primary hues and subdued pastels are frequently used in whimsical ways in Anderson's color schemes. The color selections inspire a sense of nostalgia in the spectator, which not only sets the mood but also feels both familiar and fantastical. Anderson's predilection for symmetry and centered compositions forms a signature rhythm to his scenes. He's often looking for particular compositions in all of his shots; one can often tell it's a Wes Anderson movie by a still screenshot as his compositions are so recognizable. These visual constraints, coupled with recurring themes of family dynamics, flawed characters, and intricate subplots reflect a broader narrative constraint that Anderson has embraced. Each film, though unique in storyline, feels intrinsically "Andersonian", showcasing how constraints, derived from a strong creative vision, can forge a signature style.

Renowned Architects Zaha Hadid and Frank Gehry similarly work within the bounds of their distinct visions. Hadid, known for her fluidic structures, often drew inspiration from natural landscapes. Her designs are freeflow at surface level, but they adhere to constraints of spatial flow, organic continuity, and integration with the surrounding environment. Glasgow's Riverside Museum is a wonderful example of Zaha Hadid's concept of architectural fluidity, with its looping roof and zigzagging walkways that mimic the flowing waves of the adjacent river. Conversely, Frank Gehry is renowned for his deconstructivist architectural approach, which produces projects that appear both harmonious and broken. The Guggenheim Museum in Bilbao's interlocking volumes clad in titanium may initially appear chaotic. A closer examination reveals Gehry's limitations, though: a play with light and shadow, a conversation between the building and its surroundings, and a dedication to designing areas that evoke wonder and reflection.

Even literature, another center of creativity, is susceptible to vision-induced limitations. From the chakra governed ninja world of *Naruto*, to the very specific political world of *Game of Thrones*. The rules that govern the fictional world create a relatability to our own and also aid the author in shaping the story and propelling it forward. George RR Martin often said that he spends a lot of his time writing his characters and getting to understand exactly how they would behave when receiving inputs. He places them in situations and with other characters and merely writes what those characters will likely do. The plot itself forms from the interactions of the characters. He often said that he didn't know where the story would go when he first started writing the books, but he knew exactly how his characters would behave.

The common thread weaving through these diverse areas is the philosophical acknowledgment that creativity often thrives in bounded spaces. Constraints, born out of deep-seated vision, act as the crucible within which raw ideas are forged into masterpieces. They provide a structure, allowing artists to delve deeper, explore nuances, and challenge conventions. When we get to describing the creative process later on in Chapter 5 of this book, we'll discuss Graham Wallas and what he presented in his seminal work, *The Art of Thought*. In it, he postulates that constraints can stimulate the incubation phase of creativity, where ideas simmer subconsciously, eventually leading to illuminating insights. Constraints are at the heart of creativity. Being able to identify what your self-imposed constraints are is at the heart of finding your creative voice.

It is crucial for your own creative process to be able to self-reflect and clearly identify your senses of what you like, dislike, and why? Being able to articulate your own sense of contexts beyond the work you're creating. The delicate dance between creative vision and constraint is paradoxical to the nature of creativity. A creative vision is simply the context within which ideas can be generated.

The creative vision can take many forms, often approached from the sense of value. What kind of context will be created so that you can determine if an idea is valuable or not? Sometimes the creative vision can be pure artistic, like Cézanne wanting to make visible how the world touches us and of cultural value as he wanted to challenge what is defined as artistic norms of the time. Sometimes, however, the value could be functional, coming from the desire to have a technical break-through and achieve something that hasn't been done before.

The 2018 *God of War* of PlayStation 4 developed by Santa Monica Studio was received with widespread acclaim for its deep storytelling and complex characters as well as its technical and design innovations, which included the removal of loading screens. This self-imposed limitation wasn't just a technical feat; it was a choice that affected the game's narrative and mechanics along with every aspect of the design process that followed.

The first and most noticeable effect of this design decision was the introduction of a single continuous camera shot that follows Kratos and his son Atreus on their journey. Instead of cutting out or fading to black for a loading screen, the camera pans, zooms and rotates seamlessly around characters, environments, and action. This constant perspective offers unprecedented immersion. Players are not just observers; they are active participants in Kratos and Atreus path without artificial disruptions to the flow of emotion and story.

The lack of loading screens influenced the game's level design. The world of *God of War* is intricate, with interconnected realms and spaces. To maintain the seamless experience while allowing for vast and detailed environments, the developers used various techniques, such as having Kratos and Atreus traverse tight spaces, tunnels, very long elevator rides or engage in extended dialogues during boat rides. These moments, while serving as masked loading periods, also doubled as opportunities for character development, world-building, and lore exposition.

Narratively, this unbroken flow anchored players deeper into the father-son story of Kratos and Atreus. Each moment, whether it's a heart-to-heart conversation between the duo, a climactic battle, or the simple act of observing the world around them, contributes to the storytelling. The uninterrupted design ensures that players fully engage with the emotional weight, challenges, and growth of the characters.

The self-imposed constraint of eliminating loading screens in *God of War* 2018 wasn't just a technical showcase. It was a creative vision that served as a foundational design principle that informed the game's narrative structure, environmental design, combat mechanics, and emotional depth. The team's commitment to this vision resulted in a game that offers an uninterrupted, deeply immersive, and narratively rich experience, offer us developers a bag of tricks to try to go around an intrusive loading screen and is a good example of how the self-imposed constraints of a creative vision, even those of a technical nature, can inform and strengthen creativity.

Creativity almost always comes from operating with a deliberate set of constraints that are either imposed by the context or self-imposed in the form of creative vision. I did say almost always, however, because sometimes we don't deliberately define those constraints with purpose, but we stumble upon them.

Accidental Creativity

In the search of value for an idea, one would be defining the context and problem space in which they're operating, or perhaps the constraints as they try to ideate. While trying to find a solution to a specific problem, sometimes you may stumble upon either another solution or even another problem entirely that changes the space you were working in a second.

Alexander Fleming was a bacteriologist at St. Mary's Hospital in London. He had been running experiments on the influenza virus in the laboratory of the inoculation department, and while conducting one of these experiments in 1928, he left on a 2 week vacation.

When he returned, he noticed that mold had contaminated one of his petri dishes, which had been left out with a staphylococcus culture. He expected that mold would simply contaminate the dish, but to his surprise, he noticed that the bacteria around the mold were being destroyed, whereas the bacteria further away remained normal. That mold is called *Penicillium Notatum.*

Fleming's accidental discovery of penicillin marked the beginning of modern antibiotics, perhaps one of the most groundbreaking medical discoveries, and has since saved countless lives. The curiosity to investigate was critical to the eventual discovery, but it was definitely not planned for.

Being creative means being open to new findings and radical ideas.

Spencer Silver was a chemist at 3M who was trying to develop a super-strong adhesive. Instead, he accidentally created a low-tack reusable adhesive that wasn't at all what he set out to make. For several years, he tried to think of a practical application for it and couldn't come up with one. However, in 1974, his colleague Art Fry was looking for a way to keep the bookmark in his book from falling out. He remembered the adhesive that Silver created; he coated small pieces of paper with it, and that's how the Post-it notes were born. The good-for-nothing adhesive with appropriate design ideas became one of the most widely used office supplies in the world to this very day.

While good designers have strong intuition toward problem solving of issues, one can never know if a design is truly functioning as intended unless they test it. This is why testing and iteration are at the core of the design process. Sometimes, those designs don't work as intended, but even better and in unexpected ways. There's creativity in identifying when those moments happen and building upon them.

In the late 1970s, Tomohiro Nishikado was developing *Space Invaders* for Taito. Inspired by popular sci-fi movies of the era like *Star Wars* and *War of the Worlds*, he wanted to make a game that featured multiple enemies attacking in formation and in waves. The player controlling a land anti-air vehicle must defeat wave after wave of descending aliens from the top of the screen, and the game will be over if they hit the ground.

Due to the hardware limitations at the time, processors couldn't handle a lot of moving objects on screen at the same time, so whenever there were more aliens on screen, they moved slower. To keep the speed constant, Nishikado increased the speed at which the alien ships moved. However, as the player destroyed more and more alien spaceships, fewer were left on screen, meaning that they were descending on the player even faster.

Playing that out, Nishikado quickly realized that the increase in speed made the game more challenging and exciting the more the player progressed. A monumental game design discovery as Nishikado literally accidentally invented difficulty curves, a now basic game design principle of challenge increasing the more the player becomes adept and advances in the game. Nishikado was able to identify an opportunity in that happy accident, adapt it to make the game better, and revolutionize game design in the process.

Space Invaders was eventually released in 1978 becoming an instant success and a gaming culture icon. It is rumored that there was a shortage of 100 yen coins (commonly used for arcade machines of the era) due to the game's insane popularity. The game remains engaging and challenging to this day, and difficulty curves have since been adopted and expanded upon by nearly every video game, a fundamental aspect of game design in its own right.

While testing *Street fighter II*, producer Noritaka Funamizu noticed that, under certain conditions, it is possible to chain multiple attacks in a row that would not allow the opponent to recover in time to block. That usually happens when one player is able to land two attacks or more while the other character is still in the damaged animation from the previous one. This was not an intentionally designed feature and was, in fact, logged as a bug.

They eventually decided not only to keep it as a feature, but to add a counter to how many consecutive attacks can you land before your opponent blocks, and named it the combo system.

Once *Street Fighter II* released in the arcades, players started discovering and exploiting this feature, using it to release devastating sequences of attacks. Their ability to execute those combos added a layer of depth and skill to the game, which in turn set ablaze the competitive scene around the game. The combo system is not only a staple mechanic of all subsequent *Street Fighter* games but also of every fighting game that has come out since, influencing the development of the genre as a whole.

True creativity involves sustaining the original vision, but with constant evaluation and elaboration of it, openness to unexpected outcomes, and allowing oneself to develop it to its full potential.

Defining Creativity

Ultimately, the creative potential is only realized through the execution of the ideas that carry it. If there is no outcome to the thought and no human action to guide it, then an idea remains abstract in its beholder's mind.

One must produce to be creative.

If I were to summarize everything we have discussed so far, then it'd boil down to this: Creativity is not to make things; it is to generate ideas that are both original (novel, fresh, and surprising) and appropriate (fitting to a specific context), then execute those ideas to an outcome. The definition of creativity that we'll use in this book is one Margaret Boden expressed: "A creative idea is one that is novel, surprising and valuable" (Boden, 2004).

We will go through how we arrive at ideas generally in the following chapter on inspiration. We will then discuss how we arrive at and evaluate originality and value in the subsequent chapters.

Further Reading

Alexander, L. (2023). *Road to the IGF: Lucas Pope's Papers, Please*. Game Developer. https://www.gamedeveloper.com/design/road-to-the-igf-luca s-pope-s-i-papers-please-i-

Andreasen, N. C. (2006). The creative brain: The science of genius. Penguin.

Astbury, J. (2022). *Daniel Libeskind's Jewish Museum is a "foreboding experience*." Dezeen. https://www.dezeen.com/2022/05/20/daniel-libeskind-jewish-museum-deconstructivist-architecture

Bennett, J. W., & Chung, K. T. (2001). *Alexander Fleming and the discovery of penicillin*. Pp 163–184.

Boden, M. A. (2004). *The creative mind: Myths and mechanisms*. Routledge.

Bois, Y. A., & Krauss, R. (1998). *Cézanne: words and deeds*. October, Vol. 84 pp. 31–43. The MIT Press

Darwin, C. (1859). *On the origin of species: Facsimile of the first edition*. Harvard University Press.

Darwin, C. (1900). *The life and letters of Charles Darwin*. D. Appleton.

Eyvazi, M., Alaeddini, M. A., & Nickfam, R. (2015). A Structural Approach to God of War, a Video Game by Santa Monica. *International Journal on Studies in English Language and Literature*. July pp. 5–15.

Fine, G. (1993). *On ideas: Aristotle's criticism of Plato's theory of forms*. Clarendon Press.

GLä Veanu, V. P., & Gillespie, A. (2014). Creativity out of difference: Theorising the semiotic, social and temporal origin of creative acts. In *Rethinking creativity*. Routledge, pp. 1–15. https://www.taylorfrancis.com/chapters/ edit/10.4324/9781315866949-1/creativity-difference-vlad-petre-gl%C4% 83veanu-alex-gillespie

Heath, C., & Heath, D. (2017). *The power of moments: Why certain experiences have extraordinary impact*. Simon and Schuster.

Henderstot, S., & Lapetino, T. (2017). Undisputed Street Fighter: The *art and innovation behind the game-changing series*. Dynamite Entertainment.

Kottler, M. J. (1974). Alfred Russel Wallace, the origin of man, and spiritualism. *Isis*. 65(2), pp. 145–192.

Koyama, Y. (2023). Arcade Games (1): From Elemecha to Video Games: The Birth of *Space Invaders* and the Establishment of the Arcade Game Industry. In *History of the Japanese Video Game Industry*. Translational Systems Sciences, vol 35. Springer Nature Singapore.pp. 15–25.

Lehrer, J. (2008). *Proust was a neuroscientist*. HMH.

Perron, B. (2012). *Silent Hill: The terror engine*. University of Michigan Press.

Plato. (1943). *The Republic*. Legend Press Ltd.

Rabinow, R. A., Druick, D. W., & di Panzillo, M. A. (2006). *Cézanne to Picasso: Ambroise Vollard, patron of the avant-garde*. Metropolitan Museum of Art.

Seitz, W. (1957). *Nature and abstract painting*. Brooklyn Museum Bulletin, pp. 7–12.

Tinterow, G., & Loyrette, H. (1994). *Origins of impressionism*. Metropolitan Museum of Art.

Chapter 2
Inspiration

Creativity is a wild mind and a disciplined eye.

– Dorothy Parker

As I mentioned before, I have taught game design in different schools around the world, from the Middle East to New Zealand, to Japan to Europe to North America. I have had students from so many different backgrounds and walks of life. Usually, if I'm giving an extended course or a game design 101 course, I spend quite a bit of time doing exercises with the students as well as going through the theory. My philosophy is that I would ask them to do the exercise, and then as I present the theory, it'll help them reflect on their own thought process, and then something will light up. They will gain an understanding of how the theory takes shape in their own thought process. That in turn helps them better understand themselves, and become more open to adapting additional parts of the theory they were just presented.

One of the exercises that I would do is that I would ask the students in my class to have a quick think about their lives—I usually time it to 10 or 15 minutes tops—and list down general ideas or directions that would make an interesting video game. Then, once they're done, I would ask volunteers of them to read out what they had in mind, the rest of the students could ask them questions or comment or have a joke around. I had several observations doing this exercise globally.

The first is that almost every single time I did this, as one student was talking about their ideas, others would say, "I was thinking of the same thing" or "I had a very similar idea". There was always a passion

DOI: 10.1201/9781003261834-2

about how unique their idea was and how much they wanted to leave their job to pursue this idea, only to find out seconds later that someone else in the same class has had a very similar idea. This is a recurring theme that I have observed even with professional game developers. Many times, as I'm reviewing either game pitches from teams or specific feature pitches, they are very similar to something else another team has pitched within a very short time period. Sometimes we are working on developing a game concept, and another very similar game from a studio on the other side of the world gets released. So from observation A here, it is very likely for two people to have the same idea. It happens all the time.

The second observation that I had is that in every single class, no matter where in the world we were or people's backgrounds, there were recurring ideas, or more to say categories of ideas that showed up in every class, and oftentimes multiple times in the same class. There was almost always a game idea around cooking, travel, commuting, raising the kids, or sports that people play. As people presented their ideas, they would say something like, "I love cooking so I thought I could turn this into a video game." In many of those common categories of ideas, people wanted to create games based on activities they enjoy doing regularly.

What we do inspires us.

The more we are captivated by something in our lives, activities we do or culture that we consume (music, books, games, plays, movies, etc.) they will somehow find their way subconsciously into our works of creation. It would make a lot of sense that if we spend a lot of time doing something that stimulates us so much—like traveling for example—then it will find its way to our creations. This even became more apparent to me when I was teaching those classes remotely during the COVID-19 pandemic in 2020. That was when some categories, like travel or commute, disappeared completely. No one had ideas for games about these things anymore. However, other categories of game ideas appeared instead. A lot of them were around contact tracing or games about avoiding other people in the grocery store.

If creativity—as we concluded in Chapter 1—is to generate ideas that are both original and valuable, increasing the rarity or unlikeliness of an idea to occur is an important aspect of arriving closer to originality. We can't be novel if we all keep coming up with similar ideas all the time. If what we do regularly inspires us, the media that we read, watch, or even play will inevitably show up in our creative work. Then, how do we choose what inspires us? Why do some ideas inspire us whereas others don't leave a lasting effect on us? Understanding what inspiration even is becomes a vital part of arriving at originality.

Defining inspiration

The word "inspiration" itself comes from the Latin word *inspirare*, which means to breathe into. It is often defined as a sudden outburst of creativity or being suddenly mentally stimulated and therefore driven to do something, especially creatively. Inspiration is a moment during which we witness something, hear someone speak, observe a natural phenomenon, take part in an activity, or even have a dream and be overwhelmed with an empowering sense of creativity. Ideas start racing in our head, and every inch of our bodies is urging us to start doing or to start creating.

These moments appear to just show up randomly; even in ancient times, it was believed that the gods bestowed inspiration on selected individuals through various means and spoke through them in their acts of creation. In fact, many times, it was believed that creatives were not acting out of having talent of their own but because they were selected by higher forces. Plato even once described poets as being "possessed", being in a state of mental frenzy or trance during which rhymes came out of them without any control of their own.

The Greeks believed that inspiration came from muses, a category of goddesses that inspire creation by bestowing knowledge on fortunate individuals. Legend has it that Osiris recruited nine muses—the nine daughters of Zeus—before embarking on a world tour of sorts to spread knowledge, dance, poetry, and the arts across the lands.

The nine muses had different areas of speciality. In Calliope (epic poetry), Clio (history), Euterpe (music), Thalia (comedy), Melpomene (tragedy), Terpsichore (dance), Erato (love and lyric poetry), Polyhymnia (hymns and sacred poetry), and Urania (astronomy), it is said that a muse graces inspiration of those who evoke them through study, remembrance, or when being invoked. It's asking for help in inspiration from the muse or inviting them to speak directly through the invoker.

In Norse mythology, Odin, the Allfather, is referred to as the god of inspiration. As he never kept knowledge to himself, Odin inspired others by sharing his knowledge. When people obtained knowledge within themselves, they were driven to act on it and therefore create. Odin wanted to use his wisdom and knowledge to change and morph the world. It was by spreading knowledge that he inspired people to carry out further acts of creation.

In the 16th century, Italian painter and architect Giorgio Vasari in his book *The Lives of Artists* attributed artistic talent and inspiration to that of divine power. He praised Leonardo Da Vinci's paintings as coming "from god" and even proclaimed that sculptor Michelangelo Buonarroti had a mission from the heavens to show mankind god's perfection in design.

After the 17th century, there was a noticeable acceleration in scientific advancements and creativity that resulted in rapidly expanding human technology. Perhaps as people were using that technology to discover and invent things, they started to attribute the inspiration more to their own work and less toward the divine. I expect that humanity started to understand themselves and the world around them even better and in turn moved to believe that inspiration comes from within. Albert Einstein described it as a "sudden illumination" in the brain, a sudden realization within a reflective or observational moment.

Swiss psychiatrist and psychoanalyst Carl Gustav Jung's theory of inspiration see inspiration as an entirely internal process. It was more about self-discovery, transformation of personality traits, and maturation of thoughts and ideals that can be stimulated through external triggers (what we see or do), thus fueling personal drive toward action (e.g. to create). The journey of self-discovery is one toward individuality, the realization of the self. Where one would explore and integrate various aspects of the unconscious personal thought or understanding of life themselves. This is not just understanding one's personal history and experiences but also engaging with universal symbols (ideas in a similar way to how Plato described them in Chapter 1) and themes that resonate across cultures and time.

Jung believed that inspiration is an outcome of engaging with the unconscious; those creative ideas and insights will emerge from the depths of the mind and manifest as dreams, visions, or spontaneous thought. The individual can't really control this process, but it's something that happens spontaneously to them. They can, however, facilitate it through practices like active imagination, where they can intentionally engage and reflect on the contents of the unconscious. There we can experience moments of profound insights and inspiration, often leading to a greater understanding of ourselves and our place in the world around us.

In Jung's view, true inspiration is a window into the deeper aspects of the self and a step toward the holistic integration of one's personality. It's a dynamic interplay of consciously exploring the unconscious and aids not just in self-realization but in realizing creative potential by encountering the ideas that are deeply personal and universally resonant. Whatever source of inspiration for ideas is locked down deep within us, Jung wants us to dive deeper into ourselves and find those sources. What external triggers have affected us on a deeply personal level? What kind of universally resonant inputs did we take in and integrate as part of ourselves and how can we engage with them?

So our thoughts have evolved from praying to the gods and muses hoping for inspiration to start thinking about those external triggers. How can one find these triggers and utilize them to arrive at that given moment of sudden illumination and start creating? The external triggers that intertwine with the self are sources of inspiration.

Sources of inspiration

We take in input from so many different sources all the time—that input ends up shaping who we are as humans and our views of the world. It forms our preferences, our opinions, our perspectives, and everything else that ultimately defines us. In our constant conversations with ourselves and the universe, we find inspiration. In turn, that very conversation shapes how we create, everything that you've done, thought of or anything that happened to you until the moment you struck a brush stroke on a canvas and liked it, is the reason why you liked it. The cumulative experience you've had until that moment is the reason you liked that brush stroke and decided to go with it. Understanding the part of self that caused us to a true key of creative sobriety (later on that in Chapter 3).

Your sources of inspiration—whether you know it or not—shaped the very person you are and everything you create. The very person you are is why you observe and select a source of inspiration over the other.

In her seminal work *Approaches to Art in Education* (1978), Laura Chapman summarized four distinct sources of inspiration for creating art: ordinary experiences, environment, inner self, and quest for order. Those classifications some would argue extend beyond art and allow us to build on to apply to most things, from scientific ingenuity to creativity in video game development and beyond. A lot of ideas also find their source in a combination of inspiration from multiple sources, most ideas can come from the merger of different sources with our own inner self or imagination.

Ultimately, inspiration source leaves an impression on us. How we retrieve and mold that into an idea is a direct reaction to our life journey. How we use our imagination is directly connected to how the world touches us.

Ordinary experiences

What we arrived at when working with students above, what we do inspires us. Personal experience includes everything that we have in our daily lives, what we do out of habit, the people we have in our lives, and our basic needs that are shared with everyone else. Most children's spontaneous drawing falls in this category. They often will draw their parents, friends, pets, favorite food, their home, or other aspects of their lives. Perhaps some kids add a bit more to that ordinary experience, which is probably a mix of the following categories as well.

Larry David famously spoke about creating a show about nothing. He wanted to create a show about a group of people living in New York City, ordinary people with regular jobs, dating lives, and problems. He had a sensibility for awkward moments and situational comedy, with Seinfeld being the final output. One of the most popular TV shows in the world was a show in the words of its creator about "Nothing."

Games are a powerful medium of allowing the player to be in the position of someone else and live through that life. Often referred to as player fantasy, it's to create a sensation for the player to live through the experiences of someone else. The closer those fantasies resemble the everyday lives of actual people the more rooted in this source it would be. Some of the most popular video games of all time come from directly translating ordinary experiences into an interactive experience. Sports games fall into this category, FIFA—or now known as EA FC—is perhaps the most successful example of this. While most people wouldn't become professional football players in their lives, calling this an ordinary experience might be counterintuitive, but it mostly speaks to the non fantastical aspect of the experience. Most racing games such as the *Gran Turismo* series or *Need for Speed* series directly translate the racing fantasy into a video game. In more general terms, games that closely simulate experiences that we or other people have regularly would have been a result of an inspiration from this source.

Inspiration from ordinary experiences, however, can be slightly more complicated than simply simulating our experiences directly one-to-one. Oftentimes we look at our experiences and then we add what's often dubbed as our "personal twist", personal preference selecting how we merge, combine, add, or omit to form something new.

The movie *Licorice Pizza* written and directed by Paul Thomas Anderson is a great example of such a complex mixture of several experiences and real-life elements, stories, and observations. The main character, Gary Valentine played by Cooper Hoffman, is a child actor who starts a relationship with an older photographer when he was in high school. They go on to do several events that later on include starting out a waterbed business and a pinball business. Valentine was based on Gary Goetzman, a childhood friend of Anderson who was also a child actor and waterbed salesman in the 1970s in LA.

The movie is heavily inspired by real-life elements and events. The title itself, *Licorice Pizza*, is an homage to the Southern California record-store chain that existed at that time. There's a character modeled after Jon Peters, a Hollywood producer and former hairdresser, who is played by Bradley Cooper in the film. There's even an audition for a real movie titled *Breezy* which was directed by Clint Eastwood in 1973. Even the casting of the film included friends and family members of the production crew.

Alan Haim's real-life family members play her on-screen family, and Anderson's partner Maya Rudolph and their children make an appearance.

In fact, the idea of a relationship between the two main characters came to Anderson when he was picking up his son from school on yearbook day and noticed one of the other kids in line was trying to hit on the much older female photographer; he mused and wondered how that kind of relationship would've played out.

Paul Thomas Anderson combined so many real-life experiences, people from his life, and stories that he witnessed firsthand or was told to him by his close friends, as well as relied heavily on aspects of pop culture, movies, stores, and locations that he frequented to create a movie that garnered universal critical acclaim upon its release, gathering several awards and five Academy Award nominations, including Best Picture, Best Director, and Best Original Screenplay.

Natural and constructed environment

Observational work falls in this category. This is what we observe in the environment around us. Our habitats, city, neighborhood, personal space, and travel observations among many others. These are the observations we made as we're creating new experiences. Nature has inspired us since the dawn of time; our observation of Pacha Mama and her creations has always been a source of endless fascination as well as countless creative and scientific discoveries.

Gregor Mendel was educated at the University of Vienna where he was exposed to contemporary scientific theories and experimental techniques in psychics, mathematics, and natural science. Though he would go on to make pioneering scientific contributions, those would only happen during his time as an Augustinian monk at St. Thomas Abbey in Brno.

His monastic commitment provided him with essential resources, namely time, space, and a well-established garden where he started conducting his experiments. In the 19th century, the scientific community was keenly interested in plant hybridization, which peaked Mendel's interest in how traits are passed from one generation to the next. He picked pea plants because they had clearly distinguishable traits, were easy to cross-breed, and had a short generation time, making them ideal for his studies.

Mendel's experimental approach had detailed records of all of his observations and then applied statistical analysis to interpret the results through his background in mathematics, which led him to formulate the laws of inheritance, later known as Mendel's laws. The father of modern genetics made pioneering contributions to the field through meticulous observation and experiments with his surrounding natural environment as his key source of inspiration but also combined with his personal journey as a mathematician.

Observation of nature has often inspired masterful creations by artists through the ages, one of the most monumental of which was a series of paintings called "Water Lilies" by our friend Claude Monet.

Monet's garden in Giverny is a thing of legend. It was a carefully cultivated space, with a wide variety of flowers and a water lily pond complete with a Japanese bridge. There Monet spent years captivated by the view and engaged his artistic sense. The series consists of approximately 250 oil paintings that were created over the last three decades of his life. It was a result of a deep fascination and connection with his natural surroundings.

Notable for their exploration of light, reflection, and atmosphere, Monet's depiction of the water lily pond varies dramatically in mood, showcasing different times of day and seasons in which he painted. It wasn't just about painting what he saw; it wasn't a representation of a garden scene, but it was to capture the ephemeral and transient qualities of nature. He wasn't painting the water lilies, but capturing the essence of the experience of seeing them.

The series also represents the personal journey for Monet. During the years he worked on these paintings, he battled cataracts and the progression of that condition was subtly reflected in his style of painting changing over time. In the later paintings, he became bolder in the use of color and less defined forms, as if his style grew increasingly free and less concerned with detail due to his eyesight struggles. The water lilies grew from direct environmental observation of nature and became a dialogue of his intimate connection to the garden in Givern, the fleeting beauty of the natural world, and his own personal life journey, making it one of the most significant contributions to art.

An example in video games comes from *The Last of Us*. Developer Naughty Dog makes use of the real-world biological characteristics of Cordyceps fungus as an inspiration for its main dystopian narrative backdrop. Drawing parallels between the fungus's real-life impact on its hosts and the fictional pandemic it triggers in the game.

In nature, the Cordyceps fungus infects its host—mainly ants—manipulating its behavior in a phenomenon known as "behavioral modification" forming a parasitic relationship. The infected insect is driven to climb up to the highest vantage point where the fungus eventually kills the host, grows out of its head, and releases its spores from a high altitude to maximize the spread.

The last of us imagines what would happen if a mutated strain of the Cordyceps fungus would infect humans and the catastrophic pandemic it would cause. In the game, infected humans become aggressive, lose their sense of self and like the ants, and eventually succumb to the fungal growth that overtakes their bodies.

The inspiration taken from the fungus in nature was followed with deep research by the developers to further instill a sense of realism in the game's world, which also heightened the horror and urgency of the main storyline. Moreover, the game uses that plot device as a means to explore deeper themes of survival, morality, and human nature under extreme circumstances that turn the world upside down. Naughty Dog drew inspiration from the horror of nature and amplified it in a way that caused us to think and ponder our actions in that light.

Observing mother nature is an endless fountain of inspiration; however, the civilizations that we built around us also count as habitats in which we live. The creations of our fellow men around us cause endless fascination either through observing other people's creations or through how those creations directly affect the way we live our lives. Those can be anything from the buildings that we inhabit or pass by, to the technology we use to get around, communicate, or simply be sources of daily interactions. Many of the elements that inspired my students came directly from their everyday activities like commute, travel, or walking in the park.

In one of his visits to Paris, designer Tinker Hatfield was fascinated by the Pompidou building in Paris, a building known for its inside-out architecture with structural and functional elements like pipes and ducts displayed clearly on the exterior of the building. Hatfield was inspired by the notion of displaying functional elements that are usually hidden on the outside as aesthetic. That led to the design of the Nike Air Max 1, where he showcased Nike's new Air sole cushioning system, which previously was hidden inside the midsoles of shoes.

The distinctive look became the hallmark of Nike Air Max Shoes but also became the design direction of future shoes, drawing inspiration from functional items and giving them more visibility. The Nike Air Max 93 was inspired by a plastic milk jug, considering how blow molding produced 270-degree visibility of the air unit. The Air Max 95 was inspired by eroding landscapes and how the strata under the earth's surface led to its gradient design.

The nucleolus of an idea can come from anywhere. It's often an observation within our environment that causes us to ponder, reflect, and be inspired. Changing the environment is one of the ways many use to get more creative, from taking a walk, or working in a cafe to traveling.

Inner feelings and imagination

Expressive and imaginative work is in this category. Usually associated with idea generation that is not immediately present to the senses, it involves the capacity to envision something in one's mind through mental visualization—the creation of an image that does not yet exist—and abstract thinking—concepts that are not based on physical or concrete experiences.

Friedrich August Kekulé's discovery of the structure of benzene is a classic example of how imagination and inner thoughts inspired a significant scientific breakthrough. Kekulé made a pioneering contribution to organic chemistry with his model of the benzene molecule. Through his presentation of the structure of benzene – a ring composed of six carbon atoms with alternating single and double bonds—there was a fundamental shift in understanding of organic compounds, as it became the cornerstone for examining aromatic compounds and their reactivity. Leading to various industrial applications such as the manufacturing of plastics, synthetic rubber, and various other pharmaceuticals.

Funnily enough, Kekulé is said to have arrived at this groundbreaking idea through a dream where he saw a snake seizing its own tail, a symbol known as Ouroboros. This dream inspired him to imagine the benzene molecule in a circular shape, and the rest is history. Dreams are not the only way for images to appear to us. Einstein famously imagined himself chasing a beam of light. It got him to wonder, what if he was to catch up to it? What would the light look like then? This was a thought experiment that led him to consider the very nature of light itself and the fixed speed limit of the universe, eventually becoming one of the inspirations for his theory of relativity. Imagination allowed Einstein a level of abstraction to conceptualize complex phenomena beyond our senses.

In the theory of relativity, Einstein grappled with the understanding of the speed of light remaining constant regardless of the motion of the light source. That observation conflicted with the then-prevailing Newtonian mechanics of gravity and acceleration. How does light behave in relation to the observer? How can gravity and acceleration become indistinguishable in certain circumstances? It meant that perhaps measurements of space and time are relative to the observer's motion. He famously imagined a person in a closed room unable to tell if the force they felt was due to gravity or acceleration. That image created a radical departure from the view that gravity is a force acting at a distance; instead, it's the wrapping of spacetime by mass.

Einstein's powerful imagination and abstract thinking led to the theory of relativity, which in turn fundamentally changed our understanding of the universe. His imagination about the behavior of light is potentially one of the most valuable insights in history. Imagination is our way to ponder what our senses take in a series of never-ending thought processes.

As a young child, Shigeru Miyamoto used to look into rainpipes on the side of buildings and wonder what was on the other side. He used to imagine that if he managed to shrink himself and go through the pipe he would come out in another world on the other side. His recollection of that imagination as a child is what ended up being the green—warp—pipes in the *Super Mario* games from the first one onwards. Mario would go into the green pipe and warp to another world that looked entirely different than the one he was in.

Miyamoto's creation of *The Legend of Zelda* was heavily inspired by his childhood explorations of the hillsides, forests, and caves around his home in the rural town of Sonobe, Japan. As a child, he would wander into forests and discover lakes, caves, and rural landscapes, which later became the basis for the expansive, explorable world of Hyrule in the Zelda series. The sense of discovery and adventure that permeates his games is a direct reflection of the wonder and curiosity he felt during these youthful explorations.

In fact, directly tapping into the childlike sense of wonder that we all had is an endless source of inspiration that greatly impacts the result of our work. Children have a sense of wonder of the world; the world is vast and endless, and there's so much of it that they're seeing and experiencing for the first time. During early childhood, the brain is rapidly developing at an astonishing rate, which facilitates cognitive flexibility, the neurological growth in children actually allows them to think in ways that are less constrained than adults, who have more formed views of the world.

In their quest to understand the world around them, children tend to encounter elements of their environment that are new and mysterious to them. They are in a constant state of learning, discovery, and amazement. As they encounter things that they don't fully understand, they will start inventing explanations coming in from their limited understanding of the world around them or fantastical stories that they make up to help them fill in these gaps, blending reality with imagination in a surreal way.

While we are a lot more set in our ways due to our years of experience and societal norms, children have way less preconceived notions about the world around them. Kids are more authentic in their curiosity and exploration, and devoid of the ingrained mental models of adults. Children are naturally playful as it's an essential part of childhood development, and during play, children experiment with different roles, scenarios, and concepts. Children's imagination enhances their sense of play, instantly creating worlds and universes around their toys and their interactions with other kids. In many ways, kids are natural game designers, constantly creating and iterating on acts of play. Miyamoto is famous for tapping into his childlike sense of wonder and translating that into the games he made; some of the most beloved gaming franchises of all time came directly from the child deep within him.

There's a children's game commonly played in Japanese schools called Tama Korogashi, which translates to "rolling a ball"; it involves rolling a ball along the ground, trying to knock over pins and other targets. The ball itself is almost as large as a 5-year-old child. Kids would team up rolling the ball along the obstacle course, often feeling some difficulty as elements stick to the ball making it more difficult to navigate.

Creator Keita Takahashi, inspired by his childhood playing Tama Korogashi created *Katamari Damacy*. In this game, players control a ball called a katamari, which sticks to objects it touches, allowing it to grow in size. As the Katamari rolls, it continues to grow in size, and this makes it able to stick to larger objects, starting from the size of a marble and growing to a size where buildings and mountains stick to it.

One of the most imaginative games of all time comes directly from Takahashi borrowing from his childhood experiences while adding a whimsical touch to the final game.

Quest for order

Careful and deliberate designs, patterns, and so on fit this category.

Order is generally found in all artwork whether it is figurative, narrative, or totally abstract in nature. Even chaos, when it has been produced intentionally, might be interpreted as a form of order. Order is the intentionality of creation; it's the contextual value of usefulness of what we want to make, often how much our end result can solve a problem. Order is understanding the context in which we create (e.g. challenge the notion of what tea bags are) and then make a response as if we're solving a problem (e.g. waterproof tea bags).

In industrial design, it is trying to find the optimal number of legs a chair can have in order for it to look the best while maintaining stability. It's the architectural foundation of how much weight a structure must endure to sustain itself, on top of which further aesthetic design intention can be applied. It's finding order in the chaos of design through the intentionality of value.

When games started becoming more sophisticated and had changing views from two-dimensional perspectives that often presented player characters from the side or an isometric perspective, the move to a three-dimensional environment caused a real challenge to designers on what they should do with the camera.

The camera is the viewpoint that the player has on the game world; it's everything that's shown on the player's TV screen or computer monitor, their window into the virtual world. If the player's character is on screen, where should the camera be situated in relation to the avatar is a challenge. How can the camera be close enough to create immersion without the player's character obstructing the view? Viewing the player's avatar in the game world is what's dubbed the third person camera. In *Mario 64*, one of the earlier 3D platforming games, developers at Nintendo imagined Mario being chased by floating characters following the player with a camera on a fishing rod.

It wasn't until *Resident Evil 4* released on the GameCube that the developers at Capcom cracked the case. By placing the camera slightly over the shoulder of the avatar, they are placed on the side of the screen instead, allowing the player optimum vision of the world while maintaining awareness of the player's positioning. Even when taking aim the camera zoomed in on the aim reticle while maintaining the character's positioning on the side of the screen. Over-the-shoulder-camera is now the standard viewpoint of third person action/adventure games that has been used across the board since.

The inspiration of treating how to view the character in the world as if you're operating an actual camera is a direct solution to a problem that eventually becomes the order of things and source of inspiration for more complex designs to come after.

The common element of the sources of inspiration discussed above is that they are all points of impact for us. Meaning that in order for us to create, we have to draw from the source of inspiration that we have already registered with us: personal experiences, observations, preferences, figments of our imagination, people we know, etc.

We can't create what we don't know.

If we have had similar experiences, then it's quite likely that we'll come up with similar ideas. Therefore, in our quest for creativity, we must widen our access to inspiration.

Widening our areas of inspiration

As part of teaching game design 101, I present the students with concepts that relate to theoretical understanding of game mechanics, captured brilliantly by Jesse Schell in his book *The Art of Game Design a Book of Lenses*. Students get to understand how to analyze any game through an understanding of space, objects, attributes, rules, skills, and probability. Then we spend some time analyzing several games through those lenses. A conclusion that is presented to the students is that by modifying, adding, or removing any of those mechanics, they will create an entirely new gameplay experience.

For example, if the game space of chess is a two-dimensional 8×8 board, then any modification to that space will create an entirely new gameplay experience. For example, making the board 9×9 or 7×7, making the board three dimensional, changing how one of the pieces move, removing one of the pieces, adding a new piece, making the board circular instead of square, etc.

I then ask the students to do a group workshop, where they're going to spend the next couple of hours redesigning the game of checkers. I explain the modern rules of checkers, then I introduce the class to a treasure chest of objects that they can use for prototyping (wood pieces, dice, paper, colored pens, sticks, cardboard, and many similar trinkets).

No matter where in the world I carry out this exercise, there's always a group of students that would declare 30 minutes in that they will want to quit everything and pursue that idea that they just came up with. The process of innovation that they just processed had them completely in love with that idea. The most common of those ideas is to make the board triangle-shaped and make checkers a three-player game. The idea they're prototyping and are completely infatuated with is the one I see in every class.

If the basis of inspiration is only the information that was given to all the students, then it's inevitable that we will have very similar ideas. We will also touch on inevitable ideas in Chapter 3 of this book.

One company I worked for had several studios in different parts of the world; each studio had a design director, one of whom was myself. Together we met up regularly as design leadership, managing over 250 designers across the company. During our time over there, we conducted several surveys in order for us to understand our designers better, and we thought that there were some interesting observations we made at the time.

Despite having a large and diverse group of designers, there were a lot of patterns. As most designers were of similar age, we found out that they grew up inspired by very similar video, games, movies, music, books, and TV shows. They all spent around 10 hours on average playing video games a week. We asked them what they were playing that year, and as expected, almost all of them played at least one of the three biggest games of that year. Even when we asked what they would've wanted to do if they weren't game designers, they mostly answered either writers or movie makers (Table 2.1).

With that number of similarities in habits and objects that we consume, we create our sources of inspiration. If we all have similar sources of inspiration, then we will inevitably start having similar ideas. That is felt in the gaming industry when a highly influential game is released such as *Dark Souls*. Because most game creators play other

Table 2.1 We surveyed our designers asking them where they come up with ideas, and those were the most common answers

Where do you come up with game ideas?	Percentage
Other games	14%
Driving/public transport	14%
Walking	13%
In bed	12%
Bathroom	12%
At my desk	10%
TV/Movies	9%
Comic books	6%
Playing a sport	5%
Couch	5%

video games for inspiration, we start to see a lot of the *Dark Souls* mechanics appear in games by other developers from different parts of the world. The same example applies for a game like *Player Unknown Battlegrounds (PubG)*. Since the likelihood of a game developer—like Brenden Greene, AKA player Unknown—reading *Battle Royale*, the dystopian horror novel by Japanese journalist Koushun Takami, perhaps getting inspired by it to make a video game about the topic, once *PubG* became mainstream, the likelihood of other developers getting inspired by the game for their own work becomes even more likely. Thus having a major impact on the industry and number of battle royale games released afterwards, eventually becoming its own genre. As we thrive toward originality, the need to arrive at ideas that are statistically unlikely become more and more present in our minds. We will be discussing the likelihood of ideas a lot more in the upcoming chapter on creative sobriety.

Personal experiences

Leaning into personal experiences as a source of inspiration transcends expression; it is a mechanism that enhances our ability to draw innovative connections between seemingly unrelated topics. Personal experiences are our creative reservoir on our journey to originality. If we rely on our own uniqueness, as no two people have the same life journey, our creative wealth is more within us than we think. As our life journey is entirely our own, no one else can replicate it. Its authenticity is, by default, statistically unique. Finding resonance in it is not through recalling external factors to ourselves but how we interpret those factors.

It's not taking inspiration from recounting the movie we liked. It's interpreting creativity through expression of *why* we liked that movie. How did that experience touch us? How can we make that visible in a way that is resonant that is reflecting a true part of who we are?

Creativity is ultimately about making connections and seeing relationships between elements that might not be immediately obvious. Personal experiences buried in memories, emotions, imagination, and thoughts, each with its unique hues, are the diamond of rough of creativity. When we draw upon these deeply personal moments, we're not just recalling events; we're engaging with a complex web of feelings, insights, and reflections that can spark original thoughts.

When we infuse our work with our personal stories, we imbue it with genuine feeling. This emotional depth can make our work more powerful and relatable, given its authenticity, forging a stronger connection with the audience. It's often the case that the more personal something is, the more universal it feels. Others can sense the authenticity and are more likely to see reflections of their own experiences and emotions, which in turn inspires them. Both Monet and Cézannedrew their masterpieces inspired by scenes from their hometowns as we covered in Chapter 1. The familiar territory was fused with their feelings about their home, creating timeless classics that captivated people who never even visited those locals. The love of home is just as present in those works of art as the love for the scenery itself.

Personal experiences can serve as a bridge between seemingly unrelated topics. Our lives are not lived in silos; they are a blend of intersecting stories and disciplines. By drawing on our experiences, we can naturally find ways to link different areas of knowledge. It's Liebskind's background influencing architectural fluency, Darwin's travels influencing his discoveries or Monet's later years influencing his technique.

In practical terms, leaning into personal experiences encourages a mindset of openness and curiosity. It's about being receptive to the lessons and inspirations that our everyday lives offer us, and being willing to view these experiences through a creative lens. This mindset not only enriches our own creative journey but also encourages others to consider their experiences as potential sources of inspiration.

Reflecting on our life journey to widen our sources of inspiration is profoundly effective, if you're looking at it from the right perspective. Can you reflect on those rare experiences and points of view—not on what we experience but on how we did so? How were our feelings and imagination were sparked by what we've been exposed to? When we deepen our understanding of ourselves and the world around us through exploring our life journey, we unlock truly unique creative connections that no one but us has access to.

Analogous inspiration

Analogous inspiration refers to the process of drawing creative ideas or solutions from fields or domains that are similar or even unrelated to the one you're working in, but not exactly the same. It involves looking at how similar problems or challenges are addressed in these areas and applying those insights or strategies to your own situation in a new and innovative way. For example, a designer looking to improve the comfort of office chairs could draw analogous inspiration from car seats as they have gone through ergonomic research and design for comfort for long periods of sitting.

What makes it so powerful is that analogous inspiration allows you to step outside of the usual boundaries of your field and bring in a fresh perspective that observes how similar challenges are approached in different contexts, especially when you can bypass your common assumptions and the "conventional wisdom" of your own field. Analogous inspiration is creativity as a result of leveraging the diversity of human experience, which leads to enhancing one's own creativity and problem-solving skills.

Analogous inspiration comes from our ability to think in analogies, or analogical thinking, which is a complex cognitive function that involves drawing parallels, making connections, and drawing conclusions between different domains. *Brain-Mind: From Neurons to Consciousness and Creativity* by Paul Thagard (2021) is a comprehensive exploration of the complex mechanisms underlying human cognition, consciousness, and creativity. The research published there outlines the stages of analogical thinking:

1. **Identification of the source and target domains:** The process begins with identifying the two domains—the source (from which the analogy is drawn) and the target (to which the analogy is applied). This involves recognizing a situation, concept, or a problem that can serve as a source of insight for the other domain.
2. **Mapping:** This is the core stage where elements, relationships, and structures from the source domain are mapped onto the target domain. It involves identifying correspondences between the two domains, even if they are superficially different.

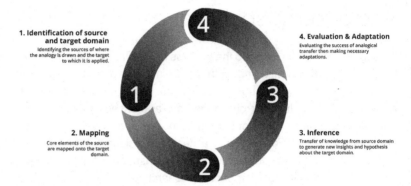

Figure 2.1 Stages of analogical thinking.

3. **Inference:** Based on the mapping in step 2, inferences are made about the target domain. This typically involves transferring knowledge from the source domain to generate new insights, hypotheses, or solutions to problems in the target domain.

4. **Evaluation and adaptation:** This is the final stage where the success of analogical transfer is evaluated, and then the necessary adaptations are made. This includes assessing whether the inferred connections are valid and useful for the target domain and making adjustments based on this evalutaion (Figure 2.1).

From a neurological standpoint, analogous thinking involves a wide-reaching network in the brain. A study highlighted in *Nature Reviews* journal on neuroscience, "The Human Imagination: The Cognitive Neuroscience of Visual Mental Imagery" (Kosslyn et al., 2013), shows that a critical part of analogical reasoning, which is visual imagery engages areas from the frontal cortex to the sensory regions which overlaps the brain's default mode network (the day dreaming network we mentioned before) The engagement of these areas suggests that they support the retrieval and manipulation of images and ideas, in other words, forming analogies.

Analogical thinking is central to human cognition, especially open-ended cognitive activity such as design. It's a broad practice to attempt to find a solution to a proposed context. You can also deduce from step one, that identification is one part, but retrieval of vital information in connection to both domains is a critical part of analogical thinking; therefore, memory is the facilitator of creative ideation when it comes to analogous inspiration. The hippocampus—vital to our memory system in the brain—is implicated and is activated as part of the valuation part. Analogous inspiration involves the generation of various ideas based on past experiences stored in memory, followed by a filtration process that retains the most innovative or useful ones. Our ability to draw on past experiences, recombine elements in a novel way then imagine and project into future scenarios and abstract concepts activates so many different regions in our brain as a fundamental part of our cognitive behavior as a whole.

So no wonder we keep running into examples of it all around us. We saw many examples of the analogous inspiration process take hold in the earlier parts of this chapter. From Hatfield coming up with a shoe design from observing architecture, to Paul Thomas Anderson creating fictional characters based on his real life friends, to the use of the Cordyceps fungus as an inspiration for the last of us. All of which came as a result of the creator looking at a field adjacent or different from their own and creating a logical connection that allows them to create in their own field.

German psychologist Karl Duncker posed a famous hypothetical problem in cognitive psychology—used to study problem-solving and creative thinking, illustrating the concept of functional fixedness and the difficulties people often face when trying to solve problems in innovative ways. It goes like this:

Suppose you are a doctor faced with a patient who has a malignant stomach tumor. It is impossible to operate on this patient, but unless the tumor is destroyed the patient will die. There is a kind of ray that can be used to destroy the tumor. If the ray reaches the tumor all at once at a sufficiently high intensity, the tumor will be destroyed. Unfortunately, at this intensity the healthy tissue that the rays pass through on the way to the tumor will also be destroyed. At lower intensities the rays are harmless to healthy tissue, but they will not affect the tumor either. What type of procedure might be used to destroy the tumor with the rays, and at the same time avoid destroying the healthy tissue?

While you're contemplating a solution to the problem, here's another story to aid your thinking.

There once was a general who needed to capture a fortress in the middle of a country from a brutal dictator. If the general could get all of his troops to the fortress at the same time, they would have no problem taking it. Plenty of roads that the troops could travel radiated out of the fort like wheel spokes, but they were strewn with mines, so only a small group of soldiers could safely traverse any one road. The general came up with a plan. He divided the army into small groups, and each group traveled a different road leading to the fortress. They synchronized their watches and made sure to converge on the fortress at the same time via their separate roads. The plan worked; the general captured the fortress and overthrew the dictator.

Have you saved the patient yet? If not, here's another story to help you out while you're still thinking.

Years ago, a small-town fire chief arrived at a woodshed fire, concerned that it would spread to a nearby house if it was not extinguished quickly. There was no hydrant nearby, but the shed was next to a lake, so there was plenty of water. Dozens of neighbors were already taking turns with buckets throwing water on the shed, but they weren't making any progress. The neighbors were surprised when the fire chief yelled at them to stop and to all go fill their buckets in the lake. When they returned, the chief arranged them in a circle around the shed, and on the count of three, he had them all throw their water at once. The fire was immediately dampened, and soon thereafter it was extinguished. The town gave the fire chief a pay raise as a reward for quick thinking.

Only 10% of people solve Duncker's radiation problem initially. However, once presented with the fortress story, about 30% solve it and save the patient. With the fire chief story added to the mix, over 80% saved the patient and solved the problem.

The answer is that the doctor could direct multiple low-intensity rays at the tumor from different directions, leaving healthy tissue intact but converging at the tumor site with enough collective intensity to destroy it. Just like how the general divided up the troops and directed them to converge at the fortress or how the fire chief arranged neighbors with their buckets around the burning shed so that their water could converge on the fire simultaneously. What this shows is that with every analogy presented from a different domain, the number of problem solvers is tripled. This also means that the more experiences or knowledge in adjacent fields we have access to, the more powerful our ability to connect those experiences and create analogues.

David Epstein, in his 2019 book *Range: Why Generalists Thrive in a Specialist World* states a case for how a breadth of experiences enable the creation of analogies, which in turn becomes a key tool in your belt for innovative problem-solving and excellence in any domain. Interdisciplinary connections are not just beneficial but essential for breakthrough thinking. Generalists with diverse backgrounds are naturally positioned to bridge gaps between many fields. They are not bound by the conventional wisdom of one field as specialists are, which lends them the freedom to approach problems from various perspectives and enables out-of-the-box thinking.

There are many successful individuals and innovators who specialized later in life after exploring a range of interests. That period of exploration gave them a rich repository of experiences and knowledge that they can later draw from in their creativity. The richer the range of experiences, the more likely for analogies to form, which in turn can lead to domain excellence and innovative breakthroughs.

Gunpei Yokoi initially worked as a maintenance man in Nintendo's playing card factory; the company was known at the time for making toys and playing cards. He obtained a degree in Electronics from the university of Kyoto and joined the company in 1965. His job was to maintain the manufacturing equipment that created hanafuda cards. But by the mid-1960s, the domestic playing card market was declining, and the company searched for new sources of profit. Experimenting with various product lines, the company began to focus on children's toys. Its president Hiroshi Yamauchi, the great-grandson of Nintendo's 19th-century founder, asked Yokoi to design "something great" for the company's fledgling games division. Yokoi's Ultra Hand, a wood lattice that extended and grabbed when users brought its handles together, was an instant hit, and 1.2 million were sold.

Yokoi then joined the company's R&D department and designed a series of successful toys, including the Beam Gun, the predecessor to the "zapper" included with NES consoles later on. As he became head of Nintendo Research & Development 1, his department focused on creating handheld games. Yokoi's inspiration came from a train trip when he saw a rider passing time by pressing the keys on a liquid-crystal display (LCD) calculator. Yokoi realized he could use LCD technology to satisfy an untapped market for portable games. By creating a device small enough to fit in your pocket and running one game, he ended up developing 60 of them for a product line called *Game & Watch*. To keep the small surface uncluttered, Yokoi created a cross-shaped directional button, or D-pad, that would become a standard feature of all Nintendo video game controllers and an industry standard for gamepads of other manufacturers as well.

Yokoi's best known innovation was the Game Boy, which combined the portability and monochrome LCD display of the *Game & Watch* with the cartridge system and 8-bit processor of the NES. Instead of making the most powerful handheld on the market, Yokoi designed the machine with a simple black and white screen because he knew that consumers would rather have something less powerful but with better battery life and more affordable price. Nintendo would eventually sell over 100 million Game Boys and is still widely considered one of the most successful video game hardware ever. From heavy machinery, to toys to sophisticated electronics, Yokoi drew from his wide set of experiences to develop products and games so beloved. Demonstrating that creativity and innovation often comes from broad and integrative thinking.

Guided by his father from a very young age, Tiger Woods is often the poster child for early specialization. His journey in golf started at the remarkable age of 2 years old when he appeared on television showcasing his golf skills. He was completely immersed in the sport, spending hours practicing, competing and studying other players, leading to his eventual extraordinary success. Wood's various accolades including numerous awards, major championships and a dominant career seem to validate the approach of intense, early specialization in a single field.

On the other hand, Roger Federer had a different path to becoming one the greatest tennis players of all time. He didn't focus solely on tennis from a very young age, but as a child, played a wide range of sports, including soccer, basketball, and skateboarding. It was only when he got to his early teens that he switched his focus, which was late compared to his peers. Federer's exceptional hand-eye coordination, fluid movement, and strategic thinking are often attributed to the wide range of activities and sports he engaged in during his formative years.

Specialization might be beneficial in a more stable and predictable field (like golf, where the environment and tasks are somewhat consistent), whereas a generalist approach is often more advantageous in complex and changing environments (like tennis, where players must adapt to different opponents, surfaces, and conditions). Mastery of the skill set requires hard work in both, but a range of expertise allows for more analogies to be formed and new heights of excellence to be developed. There are many examples of this in the video games industry as well.

Ken Lavine started out his career in screenwriting and playwriting, with a degree in drama from Vassar College. He did a short stint at a tech startup as well as wrote a couple of screenplays. Levine transitioned into the games industry in the mid-1990s by joining Looking Glass Studios working on projects like *Thief: The Dark Project*. His experience in drama and writing enabled him to infuse a unique storytelling quality into his games, setting the stage for his most notable work: *Bioshock*. A critical and commercial success, it is a culmination of his diverse experiences and interests.

Similarly, Miyamoto didn't start his career with a clear focus on video game design; he initially aspired to be a manga artist, his artistic skills are not just limited to drawing as he has a passion for music, playing the banjo, guitar, and various similar string instruments. Miyamoto's love for music, art, and whimsical characters has had a profound effect on how he makes video games. Miyamoto was able to create experiences that resonated with players on multiple levels, as his diverse interests helped him blend several arts into one with technology, creating worlds and games loved by millions around the world.

After graduating high school, Will Wright studied architecture at Louisiana State University for around 2 years. He then switched to studio Mechanical Engineering in the same school, with particular interest in robotics, space exploration, military history, and language arts. Two years later, he moved to New York City to study at "The New School". There he bought himself an Apple II and learned BASIC, Pascal, and assembly programming languages and started to get fascinated with the emerging field of game development. One year later, he moved back to his childhood home of Baton Rouge, where he spent 5 years total of collegiate study without a degree, but gained a range of experience in different fields.

During his architecture studies, Wright was influenced by the book *Urban Dynamics* by Jay Wright Forrester (1970), whose ideas on modeling cities and understanding the interactions between different urban elements shaped his understanding of urban planning. Wright was also inspired by a map editor he created for a game called "Raid on Bungeling Bay". He found that he enjoyed creating the maps—the cities and their infrastructures—more than the actual game itself. This enjoyment sparked the idea of designing a game focused solely on building and creating rather than destruction—an idea for a game that would allow players to experiment with their own urban designs and witness the outcome of their decisions.

Upon its release, "SimCity" was met with critical acclaim and commercial success. Spawning numerous sequels and inspiring countless other simulation games till this very day. The concept of a non-goal-oriented game where players could build and explore without explicit objectives was unconventional at the time and was therefore met with great enthusiasm from the players. The game's open-ended, sandbox-style gameplay was revolutionary and established Will Wright as a well-known figure in the video games industry.

Expanding areas of interest and expertise allow for more chances of analogous inspiration, therefore greatly widening our ability to generate creative ideas. Those ideas are the magic link that seems to connect two or more complex and seemingly unrelated things to a groundbreaking solution. The moment this connection happens is widely referred to as the Ah-ha moment or Eureka moment, famously attributed to the ancient Greek scholar Archimedes. According to legend, Archimedes was tasked with determining whether a crown was made of pure gold without damaging it. While taking a bath, he noticed the water level rise as he got in, and suddenly realized that the volume of water displaced must be equal to the volume of the part of his body he had submerged.

This insight led him to devise a method to determine the crown's density, thereby solving the problem. It's said that he was so excited by this discovery that he ran through the streets naked, shouting "Eureka!" which means "I have found it!" in Greek.

A "eureka moment" refers to a sudden and unexpected discovery. The term is often used to describe the instance when a complex problem's solution becomes clear, seemingly out of nowhere. It's characterized by an abrupt realization, a moment of clarity where all the pieces of the puzzle seem to fall into place, allowing the individual to see the solution they've been seeking. In psychology, these moments are studied under the concept of insight.

Insight

A moment of insight is a pivotal juncture in human cognition, with a sudden and often unexpected clarity on complex problems or ideas. They're usually abrupt and cause an immediate sense of understanding or rewiring of understanding of ourselves, the problem at hand or even the world around us. These moments are critical for creativity and are often defining moments of our lives.

People often experience these moments as flashes of understanding that come unexpectedly, typically after periods of intense focus or even a lull when the conscious mind is not actively engaged in problem-solving and the daydreaming part of the brain takes over. The suddenness is what makes these moments so impactful, as they mark a distinct shift or a clear point of before and after in terms of confusion, contemplation or clear understanding.

When an insight occurs, the solution or realization is not partially formed but fully realized. The answer is so obvious and clear in hindsight that one would wonder how they couldn't have seen it before. The clarity is often accompanied by a sense of certainty and conviction, leaving little doubt about this newfound understanding. The fog is lifted, and the landscape underneath is revealed. Oftentimes, analogical thinking induces moments of insight.

It's noteworthy that there's usually an emotional response that accompanies moments of insight; those realizations are frequently accompanied by positive emotions such as joy, excitement, and a sense of relief. The emotional surge doesn't only underscore the significance of the moment but also contributes to the memory and impact of the insight, making it more likely to be remembered and applied.

In the book *The Power of Moments: Why Certain Experiences Have Extraordinary Impact* by Chip Heath and Dan Heath (2017), insight is defined as one of the defining moments that shape our lives. Insights are instances that deliver realizations and transformations that allow us to suddenly see the world differently, gain a new understanding, or have a profound realization that changes our perspective and often our path forward. It's when one "trips over the truth"—a concept where an individual unexpectedly encounters a profound truth that they can't ignore. It's a moment of clarity that is compelling and often leads to a change in behavior. When someone realizes that they need to make a change in their personal life, or when an entrepreneur has a clear vision for a new venture.

One of the most famous moments of insight is that of Sir Isaac Newton and the falling apple. As the story goes, Newton was sitting under an apple tree when an apple fell on his head, leading him to suddenly conceptualize the law of gravity. Whether or not the story is entirely accurate, it has come to symbolize the moment of insight that led to Newton's groundbreaking understanding of gravitational force.

Stories that we visited before are all examples of moments of insight, from Alexander Flemming's insight that led to the discovery of penicillin to Tomohiro Nishikado accidentally inventing the difficulty curves, to the developers at Capcom deciding to count the number of hits in a combo and revolutionizing a genre in the process. All of these are a truth that was unexpectedly discovered, leading to a profound change in understanding of what we're looking at.

These examples reflect the transformative nature of moments of insight. While the context and content may vary widely, the common thread is a sudden, clear realization that changes one's understanding or behavior. These moments are powerful catalysts for change, providing the clarity and motivation needed to make significant life adjustments, solve complex problems, or see the world from a new perspective.

If insight is about someone unexpectedly tripping over the truth, can we then deliberately create moments of insight for others?

Scott Guthrie, the executive in charge of Microsoft's Azure cloud service, knew that their product wasn't very usable in its early days. So he devised a simple and elegant plan. He invited his senior managers and software architects to an off-site meeting and challenged them to build an app using Azure just as their customers would. "It was a complete disaster" (Nusca, 2021) in Scott's words, and that helped his team trip over the truth and spin it into action.

As game creators, we can design moments to deliberately create insight in the player and thus make their experience memorable. Toby Keith in creating Undertale, utilized this in letting the player decide on which route they want to take, pacifist or violent action, only to discover on their own through the game's events how they didn't need to be violent at all. Just because they assumed that video games entail fighting and defeating other characters, the game reveals that in fact wasn't the case at all. Tripping over the truth creates an instantly memorable moment and a defining moment of insight for the player.

Despite their spontaneous appearance, the conditions for insight can be cultivated. Allowing time for mental incubation, or taking a break from focused thought, can create the mental space necessary for insights to emerge. Similarly, exposing oneself to a broad range of experiences and ideas can provide the raw material from which novel connections are made. Additionally, maintaining an open mindset and being receptive to new connections and possibilities can increase the likelihood of experiencing these transformative moments. If we look back at Table 2.1, it seems that our designers were coming up with their best ideas when they were doing anything else other than work. Taking a step back and allowing for analogous thinking leads to the creation of moments of insight.

Inspiration and insight lead to creativity. The two key components to consider for the creative process are idea generation and idea evaluation. Idea generation is how ideas come to be; the strive for ideas to be more original, and we will be discussing a lot more of that in Chapter 3. Idea evaluation is considering how much the idea generated fits the context and is of value. Measuring the value of ideas is a topic we'll dive deeper into in Chapter 4.

Further Reading

Benedek, M., Beaty, R.E., Schacter, D.L. and Kenett, Y.N. (2023). The role of memory in creative ideation. *Nature Reviews Psychology*, 2(4), 246–257.

Chapman, L.H. (1978). *Approaches to art in education.* Harcourt Brace Jovanovich. Pp. 44–151

Crigger, L. (2007). Searching for Gunpei Yokoi. The Escapist.

Duncker, K., & Lees, L.S. (1945). *On problem-solving.* Psychological Monographs.

Epstein, D. (2019). *Range: Why generalists thrive in a specialist world.* Riverhead.

Forrester, J. W. (1970). Urban dynamics. IMR; *Industrial Management Review* (pre-1986), 11(3), 67.

Goel, A.K., & Shu, L.H. (2015). Analogical thinking: An introduction in the context of design. Cambridge University Press.

Heath, C., & Heath, D. (2017). *The power of moments: Why certain experiences have extraordinary impact.* Simon and Schuster.

Jung, C.G. (2014). *Analytical Psychology: Its Theory and Practice.* Routledge.

Kosslyn, S. M., Ganis, G., & Thompson, W. L. (2013). The human imagination: the cognitive neuroscience of visual mental imagery. *Nature Reviews Neuroscience*, 14(5), 349–359.

The Miscellany News - Levine '88 discusses career as game developer [online], (2010). Wayback Machine. [Viewed 2 March 2024]. https://www.miscellanynews.com/2.1579/levine-88-discusses-career-as-game-developer-1.2167708#.UPd1Wieum50

Murray, P. & Lynch, T & Rocconi, E (2020). The Mythology of the Muses. In *A Companion to Ancient Greek and Roman Music* Wiley Blackwell (pp.11–24).

Nusca, A. (2021). Inside Microsoft's plan to reconquer the world. *Fortune.* Available at: https://fortune.com/longform/microsoft-fortune-500-cloud-computing/ (accessed 22 October 2024).

Pearson, J. (2019). The human imagination: The cognitive neuroscience of visual mental imagery. *Nature Reviews Neuroscience.* 20(10) pp. 624–634

Schell, J. (2008). *The art of game design: A book of lenses.* CRC Press.

Sheff, D. (2011). *Game Over: How Nintendo conquered the world.* Vintage.

Thagard, P. (2021). *Brain-mind from neurons to consciousness and creativity.* Oxford University Press.

Vasari, G. (1998). *The lives of the artists.* OUP Oxford.

Chapter 3
Creative sobriety

> There are painters who transform the sun to a yellow spot, but there are others who with the help of their art and their intelligence, transform a yellow spot into the sun
>
> — Pablo Picasso

If creativity is the ability to generate ideas that are both original and of value, then it's safe to assume that it's a trait—much like that of intelligence—that everyone possesses to some degree or another. Does that mean that there are some people who are more capable of doing so than others? In other words, are there people who are more creative than others? The short answer turns out is: yes.

Highly creative individuals

When examining creativity, there are individuals who stand out due to their ability to produce work that is both novel and valuable, frequently and consistently. They are referred to as highly creative individuals. Understanding what characterizes them involves exploring various dimensions of their personality, thinking, behavior, and even brain structure.

American psychologist Donald MacKinnon, particularly known for his work on creativity and personality, tried to describe the personality of high creative individuals. He stated, "A truly creative individual has an image of [themself] as a responsible person and a sense of destiny

DOI: 10.1201/9781003261834-3

about [themself] as a human being. This includes a degree of resolute-ness and almost inevitably a measure of egotism" (1964). Highly creative individuals tend to believe that they are capable of being highly creative. To change the world, one must believe that they are capable of doing so. Highly creative individuals tend to generate ideas of novelty fre-quently, which means that they have a unique capacity to produce ideas, solutions, or artistic expressions that are not only new but also unexpected. Their thinking *diverges* from conventional patterns toward breakthroughs in thought. Originality alone isn't enough; their contribu-tions are also equally valuable, as they are useful, relevant, and often provide new solutions to old problems or present a new perspective that enriches the understanding and appreciation of a certain context.

Divergent thinking is the opposite of convergent thinking, which seeks a single correct solution to a problem. Divergent thinking involves thinking in a nonlinear manner, exploring various options and creating thought patterns that more often than not involve making unexpected connections of elements that seemingly have nothing to do with each other. We discussed analogous inspiration (the process of utilizing one domain of expertise that is seemingly unrelated as inspiration for another domain) at length in Chapter 2. Divergent thinking is the cogni-tive process that utilizes analogous inspiration frequently, and it's a hallmark of the highly creative individual. As demonstrated earlier, this is an ability that is supported by a wealth of knowledge and skills in their respective domain as well as knowledge of other adjacent or non-adjacent fields just the same.

Highly creative individuals then tend to have strong memories to retrieve the wealth of knowledge and deep understanding that allows them to recombine and restructure their knowledge in novel ways.

In addition to their mental capabilities, there are also common per-sonality traits that such individuals share. Key of which is openness to experience, which is also the most commonly observed among cre-atively prolific individuals. Experience could mean travel, jobs, relation-ships, books, movies bungee jumping, a walk in a park, etc. It is the will to engage and observe fully our life experience and seek more of it, which is why they have a wide range of interests, a strong sense of curiosity and a preference for novelty and variety. These traits tend to make them seek out new experiences and ideas, which ends up showing up in their creative output in the same way we discussed with the generalists before. As they embrace the new, they also embrace the risk and have a high tolerance for ambiguity. Compared to the average person, they are more comfortable with uncertainty. Through their belief of their pursuit, they are willing to follow their vision even in the face of potential failure.

Research conducted by Scott Kaufmann in a diverse sample of individuals totaling 1,035 participants found that highly creative people show greater openness to novel experiences are attracted to complexity, and display heightened aesthetic sensibilities. Their openness to experience is a predictor of creative achievement in the arts, whereas intellect is predictive of the same in the sciences.

Intelligence is the trait that was perhaps the most intensively studied especially in relation to creative thinking and problem solving. The most fascinating of which was the one conducted by Lewis Terman where he identified 1,528 gifted school children from a sample of 250,000 and followed them into adulthood with the goal of seeing how many of them made creative contributions. His findings highlighted that intelligence has a direct correlation with creativity, but only up to a certain threshold, beyond which there was no noteworthy difference. Above the IQ level of 140, other factors such as social adjustment and emotional stability come into play, but intelligence plays no further role in creative achievement.

From a neuroscience point of view, there have been several investigations into creative thinking and structural brain markers in relation to creativity. Most of those studied were conducted through the use of laboratory-based tasks and found structural differences. For instance, Rex Jung reported higher cortical thickness in medial regions of the parietal lobe in relation to better creative thinking. Meaning that there's scientific research that alludes to highly creative people having a slightly different brain structure.

Highly creative people seem to be actually wired differently. They are unconventional as well as intrinsically motivated and are characterized by a heightened sense of confidence, independence, and ambition. The idea of highly creative individuals being "different" has been common since Greek antiquity, as they thought that creative individuals were possessed or mentally aberrant. Even in modern times, the term "mad genius" is still widely used to describe creativity. Interestingly enough, separate individual researches conducted by Simonton and Kyaga have found that there are higher than average incidences of mental issues among people who practice professions that demand high levels of creativity, such as visual artists or writers.

The so-called madness-creativity link has sparked the interest of the scientific community, with several investigations and researches conducted to find correlations. The most well-studied psychiatric populations in this regard include individuals with schizophrenia, bipolar disorder, attention deficit hyperactivity disorder (ADHD), and autism. A number of studies on individuals, who are characterized by the presence of a high degree of either schizotypal or psychoticism traits, have demonstrated that they consistently perform better than their low trait counterparts on some measures of creativity. The same is true of populations who display clinical-moderate levels of top-down dysfunction, such as ADHD. In contrast, populations who are characterized by clinically severe levels of top-down dysfunction, such as schizophrenia, perform poorly on almost all measures of creativity (Figure 3.1).

What this basically means is that there's a direct positive correlation between attention deficiency and creativity, up until a certain point of impairment when it starts negatively affecting creative output.

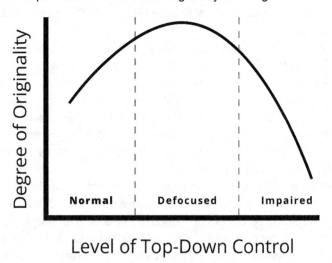

Level of Top-Down Control

Figure 3.1 Correlation between attention deficiency and creativity.

Highly creative individuals, in addition to the traits we've discussed before, tend to show some degree of mild attention deficiency. Perhaps their mind's ability to wander and daydream is what allows them to make connections between more seemingly unlikely topics which enables them to arrive more at originality. The likeliness of creating these connections—or associations—is described as associative hierarchies.

Associative hierarchies

In 1962, Sarnoff A. Mednick published a paper, titled "The Associative Basis of the Creative Process", considered to be one of the most influential works in the psychological study of creativity. This theory basically determines that the creative process is fundamentally an associative one. Our minds are filled with ideas, words, images, and symbols all linked together through our individual experience and life journey. These associations vary in strength and relevance, common associations are strong and frequently accessed, while unique and novel associations are weaker and less commonly used.

According to Mednick, each one of us has their own associative hierarchy that is completely unique to them. That hierarchy contains elements that are ordered from most common to most remote. Highly creative individuals tend to have a more flat associative hierarchy, meaning that they can access remote associations just as easily as common ones, a task that is a tad more challenging for their less creative counterparts.

The more elements we have in those hierarchies, or more experiences, knowledge, patterns, images, and ideas we have to feed that intricate network, the more associations we can make. Therefore for us to widen our areas of inspiration, the more information or *input* we take in, the more dense our network becomes. The richer our life experience is, the denser that network becomes. Highly creative individuals have far reach in their associations, but they also have a very dense network of hierarchies.

When it comes to our life experience, the more we see and experience, the more input such as images, sounds, and memories are stored in our associative hierarchy, which gives us more associative ideas that we can then reach. However, that input also causes us to contemplate increasing the density of *ideas* within us. Allowing for even more associations and creativity to occur in our work through analogous inspiration. Those seemingly unrelated concepts or ideas connect and allow us to see the world in an entirely new way. The more remote those associations are, the more likely we are to arrive at originality.

Mednick developed a psychological test to measure an individual's potential for creative thinking and ability to form associative connections, called the Remote Associates Test (RAT). Participants are presented with sets of three words—known as triads—which don't have any immediate apparent connection. Participants are tasked to come up with a fourth word that connects with each of the three words in the triad to form a common compound word or phrase. For example, given words like "Cottage", "Swiss", and "Cake", the participant should identify "Cheese" as the word that forms a logical association with each in the triad. As simple as this sounds, it requires you to navigate through your network of associations and identify a link that is not immediately apparent.

The RAT measurement considers both the accuracy and speed of the response as participants are timed and scored according to the number of correct associations made within the period of time given. Those who can make more correct answers during that time are considered to possess more creative potential or as described before a *flatter associative hierarchy* as quick access is also demonstrated especially for remote or less obvious associations (Table 3.1).

Simplicity is probably the more significant critique of RAT, as it does not accurately represent the complexity and depths of real-world creative thinking and challenges, which involve more elaborate and sustained cognitive processes. Moreover, as the test itself is linguistically based, then it's subject to cultural biases. Certain associations might be more readily apparent to individuals from specific cultural backgrounds due to the closeness of the words to the culture, but also to differences in education and language.

The speed of making connections is also debatable, as RAT greatly favors individuals who think quickly in comparison to those who are

Table 3.1 Distribution of functional RAT generated items by probability

Query no	w_1	w_2	w_3	w_{ans}	Probability
1	Exhausted	Sleepy	Weary	Tired	0.7202
2	Frame	Photo	Portrait	Picture	0.6897
3	Bassinet	Crib	Infant	Baby	0.6916
4	Daisy	Ttulip	Vase	Fflower	0.6914
5	Bulb	Dark	Dim	Light	0.5530
6	Account	Teller	Vault	Bank	0.4301
7	Cashew	Rat	Squirrel	Nut	0.3518
8	Comet	Limit	Velocity	Speed	0.2301
9	Attendance	Contemporary	Gift	Present	0.2301
10	Capability	Function	Leadership	Ability	0.1101
11	Plenty	Quantity	Site	Lot	0.0701
12	Car	Piston	Steam	Engine	0.0701
13	A	Rate	Test	Grade	0.501
14	Agent	Deception	FBI	Spy	0.0163
15	Earthquake	War	Weakness	Fear	0.0114
16	Admire	Jewel	Ocean	Beautiful	0.0111
17	Cougar	Go	Learn	Fast	0.0110
18	Burn	Flash	Pants	Down	0.0110
19	Exam	Flee	Warn	Fear	0.0110
20	Condition	Croak	Doctor	Dead	0.0105
21	Case	Fact	Threshold	Point	0.0103

more reflective in their thought process. Also, the test assumes that the connection between those words must be one correct answer, which goes against the divergent thinking that forms remote associations to begin with. There could be many different answers to the question and the speed limits the creative potential and finding many within that infinite possibility space.

These criticisms do not detract from RAT's impact, as it remains one of the most pioneering and influential tools in the study of creativity especially given how easy it is to administer and how objective the results are considering the nature of the scoring system within. It is still one of the best practical approaches to illustrate associative thinking and it's role in the creative process.

Mind mapping

Mind mapping is a visual creative thinking tool that is commonly used to represent ideas and concepts linked to and arranged around a central concept or subject as a starting point branching outwards. This creates a diagram used to visually organize information, especially in environments such as brainstorming sessions (more on that later in Chapter 4) where ideas are generated rapidly at high numbers. It's a technique that initially gained popularity in education before it found its way to business, tech, and personal planning and is a common practice in the gaming industry due to its effectiveness and elegance.

The practice was popularized in the 1970s by British psychologist Tony Buzan. He contended that traditional notes are too linear, and their sequential nature limits the brain's capacity for lateral thinking and creativity. Interestingly enough, the diagram of a mind map is similar to the brain's capability of forming associative hierarchies with the various ideas linked together in a network that bursts out of its core (Figure 3.2).

Typically, drawing a mind map starts with a single concept or idea at the centers placed in a bubble at the center. From there, branches start to radiate outwards in every direction with other bubbles that represent subtopics from the starting point, then more branches from those bubbles, and so forth. The exercise can continue for as much detail level as possible and each bubble category can have the number of branches desired as well. Some mindmaps use only words, others can include detailed descriptions or visual elements like colors, images, symbols, or video.

The beauty of mind mapping is that it encourages expansive and nonlinear thinking. It allows for the categorization of information

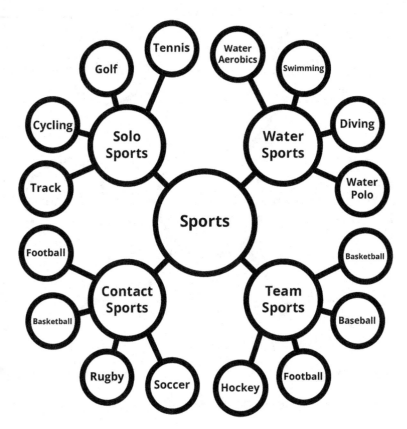

Figure 3.2 An example of a mind map, with sports being the central concept.

(e.g. having a team sports as a sub-category from sports in Figure 3.3) as it's being generated and determining at a glance the level of detail of the concept introduced. Because of that, it spurs creative thought and often leads to novel ideas or solutions to a given problem. At the very least, it helps list down all aspects that relate to a given topic that one can think of (or many in case of a group activity that generates one).

The visual side of mind maps can turn complex information into a structured and easy-to-understand diagram that helps in outlining steps, objectives, and resources that are needed when planning

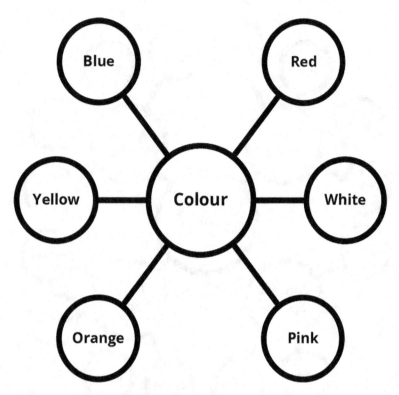

Figure 3.3 Creative sobriety example step 1.

projects. It's also a highly customizable framework that can be adapted to the need at hand.

Creative sobriety

Inspired by the RAT method I started developing my own methodology that builds on word association in idea generation but also on mind mapping methodologies to illustrate to my students how different layers of associations have different characteristics.

I start off by writing the word—for our example, here I'll use the word color—as the central idea of the mind map, then I start asking participants to say the first word that comes to mind when they hear the word color, the answers are submitted instantaneously. As I start collecting the answers they start to form the first layer surrounding color, with words like "black", "white", "red", "green", "blue", "turquaze", etc. Similarly I'll grab one of those words and now it becomes the central idea and try to branch out from there. For the sake of illustrating a point, I choose to investigate the word "white" at random. So from the word "white" in that example, I will get answers such as "wall", "shirt", "milk", "egg", "paper" and other similar things (Figure 3.4).

Using the same logic, I can take the word "milk" and get the word "cow". From "cow", I can get "horse", and then "horse" eventually leads me toward "Unicorn" (similar to the graph below). From that graph, there are many elements that we can analyze (Figure 3.5).

Highly creative individuals, with their remote association reach and flatter hierarchies, tend to skip many levels of association so they can connect "color" to "unicorn" directly as their first level of connection. Their first instinct when answering the word association question is generally to think of something that is several layers further than most people.

The circle of connections immediately surrounding the word "color" such as "red", "blue", etc. at level 1 ideas which i'm calling "inevitable ideas", those ideas are simple and straightforward connections that render those ideas statistically highly likely. The logical connection given the context of the exercise and word is so direct, that most of those associations are ones that a person inevitably will arrive at. They are

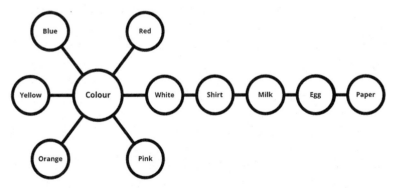

Figure 3.4 Creative sobriety example step 2.

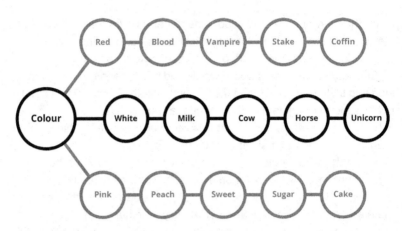

Figure 3.5 Creative sobriety example step 3.

the associations that we all normally have in our hierarchies or ones that have a high probability of existing in most people's hierarchies.

Those include information that we classify as general knowledge (such as knowledge of the colors red, blue, yellow, black white, etc) or life experiences that we all tend to have, like waking up, going to work or school or having food. The information itself is commonly obtained by a lot of people therefore, is likely to be readily available within associative reach for most individuals (Figure 3.6).

Inevitable ideas are time to market ideas. Meaning that because their level of likelihood is quite high, then it means if an idea doesn't exist on the market, it will inevitably get released. So if your idea is "pink" and that's not on the market already, then you better start making it. Most probably, several other people will be working on it as you're currently thinking about it. Most students comment in this exercise that it's easier to go first and give answers, as most inevitable ideas aren't on the board yet, and that the exercise becomes more difficult the more people I ask, sometimes I even skip a participant to the one after if they don't give a fast enough answer as the readiness of the association is a key measurement that I'm looking for.

What we described in Chapter 2 of this book about game developers being inspired by similar sources of inspiration is closely connected to this. It's the connection between the several layers of reasons for the idea to come to place and the likelihood of each. The odds of someone

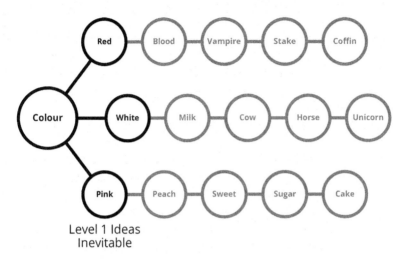

Level 1 Ideas
Inevitable

Figure 3.6 Demonstrating inevitable ideas.

being a game developer, but also wanting to read Takami's battle royale and also wanting to make a game about this topic is not trivial but quite high. It would've been inevitable that someone would've eventually wanted to action an idea that revolves around making a battle royale game.

If that source of inspiration is even more popular—e.g. more people have seen it—then the odds of works of creation based or inspired by it becomes even more likely.

A friend of mine who is a game developer was watching a popular show on Netflix one day, *Squid Game*, which is a South Korean survival drama series. The show is about a competition where 456 players who are all in deep financial debt are invited to play a series of children's games with life-threatening consequences to win a large cash prize. Each game is a traditional Korean children's game such as *Red Light, Green Light*, but with death as a consequence of losing. As the show progresses, the contestants navigate through the games, alliances form, strategies are devised, and every decision can lead to drastic consequences. The show garnered huge attention, becoming one of the most watched shows in Netflix history.

As he was watching the show, he thought to himself that if he made a video game based on the show or at least the traditional Korean games that the show is based on, it'd be a great hit especially given the popularity of the show. He was highly driven by the idea and almost started putting together the designs for his first app. Then he stopped and thought to himself, that perhaps it's better if he checks first if there are any other apps out there that are similar to the one he's about to start making.

Not only were there thousands of apps already available on the app stores. In that month, seven of the top 10 free apps on Google Play Store were related to the show and so were 6 out of 10 for the Apple app store. There were so many apps submitted that store curators had a temporary ban on submission of any new squid game app. The combination of elements leading to the idea was just very likely, given the popularity, how many developers could've seen the show and wanted to make a game about that experience? Quite a few, turns out.

Creative sobriety is a practice of reflection, to try to identify the source of inspiration, reasoning or combination of thoughts that lead to the development of an idea and try to identify at what level the idea is at. It is the phrase I put together and the main concept that I'm putting forward to you dear reader in this book.

While highly creative people can naturally arrive at connections and associations that are so far away in a reasoning perspective, with practicing creative sobriety you can intellectually push an idea further—or deeper—in levels of association and achieve a higher likelihood of being original. "Creativity is not a talent. It is a way of operating" said John Cleese (1991). The English comedian and frequent creativity speaker suggests in this quote that creativity isn't an innate ability but rather a mode of behavior that can be cultivated and developed. While highly creative individuals might naturally have a more divergent thinking style, this can also be a skill that can be developed and enhanced through practice. Techniques like brainstorming, free writing, and maid mapping are often used to do exactly that.

All of those techniques we will be discussing at various parts of this book, as we touched on mind mapping in this chapter and will talk about brainstorming in a lot more detail in Chapter 5.

Beyond techniques, however, creative sobriety advocates for reflection and self-understanding. Fostering divergent thinking comes from encouraging curiosity and exploration. As illustrated in Chapter 2, learning about a wide range of subjects, asking questions, and seeking new experiences, the breadth of the knowledge and diversity of thought expands, which provides access to diverse sources of associations. The more you learn, the more you experience, and the more resources you have. The more you reflect on who you are, how you understand those learnings, and what your thoughts are the more you form concepts that are more unique to you. Creative sobriety is the practice of trying to identify where those ideas are within you.

Creative sobriety is your ability to differentiate between a concept, and how that concept touched you. Then you achieve originality by an act of creation guided by that impression.

To be more creatively, sober means that you need to better understand yourself. That means that you need to spend a lot more time with your thoughts, not with inputs (information that feeds your associative hierarchies like reading a book or watching a movie). Spending more time with your understanding of the world and how that affects what you do. It's spending time understanding your preferences and being able to articulate or at least ponder, why do you have that preference? Then develop your ability to articulate it.

So to develop creative sobriety is to be armed with curiosity and then delve into a Jungian journey of self-discovery. Mindfulness practices and reflection may contribute to that journey. Practices such as meditation can help in clearing the mind of clutter and reduce cognitive biases to more free ideas. Outside of mindfulness, spending time with friends or family, talking to mentors or people you respect, or even talking to a professional coach to help you organize your thoughts towards reflection. The goal is to promote a more open and less judgemental mindset. As you reflect on your life journey and get fully acquainted with the core of who you are, that inspires you.

Cross-disciplinary collaboration is a great way for us to better understand ourselves and life around us. It introduces us to new ideas and perspectives that we may not have thought of from different fields, and if you couple that with *diverse* cross-disciplinary teams, people who come from different walks of life and unique knowledge and ideas, such collaboration encourages the blending and recombining of ideas, which leads to the creative approach to the work at hand.

It's scientifically proven that more diverse teams make better products, and through our exploration of inspiration and divergent thinking, we have also demonstrated how that positively affects creativity by widening our exposure to concepts and ideas that are not directly available to us.

Reflecting on your experiences, knowledge, feelings, ideas, perspective, and understanding sparks creativity. Whether through journaling, discussions, or quiet contemplation, creative sobriety is achieved through reflection and continuous growth.

The previous anecdote I shared about my friend who wanted to make a squid games app. He watched the show and wanted to make a game about the show. That's inspiration driven from a direct input (watching the show). By practicing creative sobriety, he could've asked himself what aspect of the show drove his inspiration? What made that show so captivating for him? Which part of his life journey from childhood to the point in time he watched the show was impacted when he viewed it? What would a game about those feelings be like? What would a game that embodies that part of his life be like? It may be a common experience for a lot of game developers to have watched a popular show and they wanted to make a game about the show. But it's a lot less common for game developers who watched a show and wanted to make a game inspired by the specific part of their lives that the show resonated with.

I was also inspired by Miyamoto or Takahashi and their ability to recall a part of their childhood as a source of inspiration, creating a game or a part of it that was inspired by their younger selves. So I started conducting an exercise with my students and designers, asking them to think of ideas that are inspired by their childhood. So as with other exercises, certain categories of ideas started emerging in all classes regardless of where in the world we are because they are common experiences that we all had as kids; they were mostly around games we played with other kids in the playground or at home with our siblings. For instance, every class had multiple ideas that come from "hide and seek" or other popular games like "the floor is lava" or "happy sack races".

However, there was always that one student that had a different experience. One time I had a student in Jordan. She said that as a kid, her family's apartment was on the top floor of a hospital. She recounted many experiences from her childhood walking around the wards of the hospital and being friendly with the nurses there., She thought that might make an interesting backdrop of a game. There was this other student in a class I taught in Berlin. In his childhood, he studied in a school in the countryside that was built on top of an old graveyard. He recalls that he used to tag along with his friends during recess or after school and dream up all those spooky adventures that they used to imagine on the school's premises. He thought that it would make an interesting backdrop for a game.

Originality at its heart is playing the odds game. How likely is it for someone to watch top gun and want to make a dogfighting game that's based on it? Quite likely. How likely is it for someone to grow up on the rooftop of a hospital then grow up to be a game developer then deciding to make a game about that experience? Quite unlikely. The more unlikely you "push" the combination of elements that lead to creation, the more likely you are to arrive at originality (Figure 3.7).

I also had a student in Tokyo once. She had an idea for a game around being on the metro. As I mentioned in earlier chapters, when I conduct this exercise to come up with ideas about our everyday life, the topic of commute comes up very often as what we do inspires us. Her idea, however, was about trying to look at as many people as possible without making eye contact, and the minute that rule is broken, all the passengers on the cart turn into flaming demons and they attack the player.

So even though the nucleus of the idea or input can be quite common—commute in this case—the way we perceive it can alter the originality of it. Our unique perspective can make common things unique. Our understanding of the world and the way we translate that into what we make can drive us closer to originality.

A practice that is integral to creative sobriety is to be able to stop and take note—sometimes even literally—of our rare experiences, of our understanding of the world, our perspectives, our cultural heritage, the emotional connections we form and so many other things that we take as input and translate to understanding as we go about our life journey.

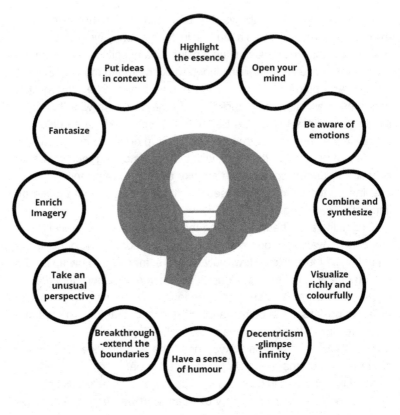

Figure 3.7 Some ideas to ponder on as you're practicing creative sobriety.

Measuring creativity

It is quite a challenge to recognize creativity in most situations for two main reasons: first, the ability of the individual to recognize or estimate their own creativity and second arriving at a consensus within a group in their evaluation of creativity as both evaluations are prone to a person's subjective opinion.

In contrast, to recognize other traits, usually tests are conducted to accurately measure and recognize said ability or trait against a metric. For instance, say your friend is claiming to have an exceptional memory, they never forget a face they say. You can devise a test to measure that, for example, have them look at photos of 50 people for a brief amount of time, then shuffle in 25 new faces and see if they can recognize who's added or not to the mix. Run that test by them and a sample of other people and determine if they can score more than the average or not to determine if their claim of memory is true or not. When presented with such facts, it's difficult to argue against the results.

See, the key aspect here, is that there is a direct measurement to go against, and that there are known facts to compare against. Therefore one can recognize if that claim is true or false. That is quite different when it comes to creativity.

As we discussed before, creativity is measured directly with the originality of the idea, meaning how new or fresh it is. Therefore, the measurement of the originality of the idea is determining how unknown it is to us. That means that we need to determine that there is no match between what we perceive and the information stored within our memory. Then we need to arrive at a unanimity of judgment as our memories and subject matter expertise differ greatly.

This often ties judgment of creativity with decision-making processes. Instead of evaluating the originality on its own, it's commonly associated with the evaluation of the appropriateness to the context as well at the same time. The recognition of both requires enough knowledge of the subject matter to know what's been done before and the overall context of which things have been created within. Therefore, in addition to subjectivity and unanimity of judgment, it's crucial to have subject matter expertise as well as part of the evaluation.

It's no wonder that measuring and understanding creativity has been a subject of research for various psychologists and scientific researchers, early in the 20th century psychologist Lewis Terman's intelligence scale introduced open-ended components that hinted at creative aspects, this paved a way for creativity to become a target of research solely for the first time in 1950s and 1960s with papers published in the topic, most pivotal of which is the one introduced by J.P. Guilford as he asserted that creativity was separate from general intelligence, leading to the development of specialized creativity tests.

Guilford divergent thinking tests

Guildford proposed a model of intellect that included a wide range of abilities, with a particular focus on divergent thinking. He defined it as the ability to generate multiple novel solutions to a problem which contrasts convergent thinking where the aim is to find a single correct answer.

The tests were designed to assess an individual's ability to produce many ideas (fluency), a variety of ideas (flexibility), original or unique ideas (originality) and elaborate or detailed ideas (elaboration). These aspects were typically evaluated as follows:

1. **Fluency:** This metric refers to the number of responses or ideas a person can generate. In other words, it measures the quantity and volume of ideas produced. A typical fluency task might ask participants to think of as many uses as possible for a common object, like a brick or paper clip, within a certain time frame. The higher the number of responses, the higher the fluency.

2. **Flexibility:** This refers to measuring the variety of categories of responses. This is a measurement of range, the participants' ability to think and demonstrate range of solution space. To riff off the previous example of the brick, if a participant presents uses of it as for building, as a paperweight or as a makeshift weapon, then they are demonstrating high flexibility. The wider the range the higher the flexibility.

3. **Originality:** You've probably guessed it. It's to assess the uniqueness or novelty of the responses. This measures the responses in comparison to other historical responses to similar tasks. Responses that are rare or unusual compared to those of the general population are scored higher on originality. The higher the score the higher the originality. A brick example would be that using bricks as a unit of currency would be more original than using bricks as building material.

4. **Elaboration:** This refers to the amount of detail in the responses. If a participant not only suggests using a brick as a doorstep but also describes how it could be painted and decorated to match the room's decor then they are showing a high level of elaboration.

The tests developed by Guilford and his colleagues typically present open-ended questions or tasks and ask participants to generate as many responses as possible. These might involve word associations, completing incomplete figures, or thinking of consequences for hypothetical scenarios. The responses are then scored according to the criteria of fluency, flexibility, originality, and elaboration. High scores of divergent thinking were the first way to measure creativity. Guilford's divergent thinking tests pioneered the field of creativity research inspiring an entire field for all the years that came after.

Naturally, as with any test, there are certain detractors and criticisms that challenge the methodology's reliability, validity, or practical applications that are worth considering as they offer a view on the inherent complexity of measuring something as sophisticated as creativity. A primary concern of which centers on the tests' overemphasis on the quantity of the ideas produced rather than their quality. Critics argue that the ability to generate a large number of ideas is not necessarily indicative of creative thinking, as the focus on generating ideas fast means that we may overlook the deeper, more nuanced aspects of creative thought.

Some researchers argue that the scores may not consistently reflect an individual's creative potential as they might not accurately measure what they intend to. Cultural bias is a significant concern here as well, the tests may not be culturally neutral, as something that can be considered origins or unique in one culture might be common in another, which leads to biased assessments in diverse populations. Scoring itself clearly demonstrates that to be able to evaluate originality, there needs to be a level of domain expertise otherwise the originality of the idea can be debatable depending on who's scoring the test. Moreover, it can also be argued that since the test-takers know that the large quantity of responses is valued they will prioritize speed over thoughtfulness, basically gaming the system and developing strategies to perform better without necessarily being more creative.

Despite these criticisms, it's undeniable that Guilford's divergent thinking tests have made a substantial contribution to creativity research with further studies and discussions about how to best define, measure, and understand creativity. The critiques have led to the development of more nuanced and comprehensive tests and models, pushing the field toward a more refined understanding of creative potential and achievement. Guilford's tests focus primarily on divergent thinking, but creativity is much broader and much more complex given that there are emotional, motivational, and contextual factors that come into play in idea generation.

Torrance tests of creative thinking (TTCT)

Developed by E. Paul Torrance in the late 1960s, the torrance tests of creative thinking (TTCT) is one of the most widely used tests to measure creative potential. It assesses creativity through tasks that involve figural and verbal activities, looking at aspects like fluency, originality, elaboration, and flexibility of thinking. The tests have been administered to individuals of all ages, from kindergartners to adults, and have been translated into over 50 languages.

TTCT is made out of two distinct forms: the verbal form and the figural form. Each of those assesses a different dimension of creative thought and expression (Table 3.2).

The verbal test contains seven subsets, each subset measures different facets of creatively thinking, those subsets are:

1. **Asking:** This subset evaluates the individual's ability to formulate questions about a specific picture or situation. Curiosity as we demonstrated so far is a critical skill for creative thinking; the ability to explore and seek out new information is vital. The individual is encouraged to ask as many questions as they can about the picture.
2. **Guessing causes:** Here, the individual is presented with a picture or a scenario and they are asked to guess the possible causes of the situation. This subset aims to test the individual's ability to hypothesize and think analytically. Exploring the different scenarios that caused the situation encourages divergent thinking and imagination.
3. **Guessing consequences:** In a similar fashion, the individual is presented with a picture or a scenario and they are asked to guess the possible consequence or outcome of the situation. This challenges the imagination and encourages anticipation as well.

Table 3.2 Different subsets of the verbal test of TTCT with descriptions and examples.

Activity	Description
1. Asking	Ask questions to know for sure what is happening in the drawing
2. Guessing Causes	Give plausible causes that lead to the action shown in the drawing.
3. Guessing consequences	List possible consequences resulting from the action in the drawing
4. Product improvement	List the most interesting and unusual ways of changing a stuffed toy elephant to make it more fun to play with
5. Unusual uses	Think about possible uses for cardboard boxes
6. Unusual questions	Propose questions about cardboard boxes
7. Just suppose	List things that will happen in an improbable.

4. **Product improvement:** This one is probably in common with most video game development job interviews, the individual is presented with a product or an object and is asked to think of ways that they can make it better. What they're looking for here usually is to test for creative problem-solving skills and critical thinking to determine the value of ideas generated.

5. **Unusual Uses:** The individual is presented with a common object (say a pot) and then they're asked for as many unusual uses for that object as possible (as a hat for example). The objective here is to test the flexibility of thinking, imagination, and divergent thinking.

6. **Unusual questions:** The individual is asked to create as many unusual questions about a picture or a scenario as possible. It encourages the test-taker to think outside the box and look at a situation from a different perspective.

7. **Just suppose:** The final subset of the verbal section asks the individual to imagine a hypothetical often fantastical situation and speculate what would happen in such a scenario. (Table 3.3)

Table 3.3 The different subsets of figural test for TTCT

Torrance Test	Starting Shape	More Creative Drawing	Less Creative Drawing
Use		Mickey Mouse	Chain
Combine		King	Face
Complete		A fish on vacation	Pot

There are three main subsets in the figural test as it evaluates non-verbal, graphic creativity. The subsets are:

1. **Picture construction:** In this subset, the examinee is given a small shape or visual cue (can be a squiggle or a zigzag, or circle) and then is asked to incorporate this cue into a larger more complex picture. They are then evaluated based on the originality, complexity, and narrative context of the constructed picture.
2. **Picture completion:** Here the individual is given several incomplete pictures or cues, and they are asked to complete these in the most imaginative way possible. Table 3.4 gives examples of what those cues could look like. The subset evaluates divergent thinking, imagination, and problem-solving skills all at the same time.
3. **Parallel lines:** In this subset, the individual is given a page with several pairs of parallel lines and is asked to create unique images or pictures using these lines as the starting point.

TTCT has been celebrated for several reasons. Its standardized nature allows for consistent administration and scoring, making it a valuable tool for research studies. It has also proven to be a reliable predictor of creative achievement and potential. The inclusion of both verbal and figural components ensures a broad assessment of creativity,

Table 3.4 Examples of starting cues for figural TTCT tests

capturing both linguistic and visual-spatial dimensions. However, it still has the criticism of Guilford's test as it can be limited by cultural and linguistic biases. While it also captures a large section of the creative process, there are aspects that it struggles to do so with including those of a more motive and motivational nature.

Though TTCT has had a lasting impact on the field and informed numerous educational programs and policies, it still lacks the ability to assess originality objectively in a way that measures it toward the appropriate context in which it's been created. The consistent need for subject matter expertise in creativity assessment across all the tests that were developed in the mid-20th century is what led to the eventual development of Amabile's CAT technique.

The consensual assessment technique (CAT)

The consensual assessment technique (CAT) is a widely respected and utilized method for measuring creativity. Developed by Teresa Amabile in the 1980s, it stands out from other creativity assessment approaches due to its emphasis on subjective judgment and its applicability across various domains and contexts. CAT is based on the premise that creativity is a primarily subjective attribute and can be most effectively evaluated through the consensus of experts within the specific domain of the work being assessed.

The core of CAT is that the assessment of creative work is most valid and reliable when conducted by experts who have an understanding and appreciation of the nuances of the domain. These experts are provided with works or responses from individuals and are asked to rate the creativity of each piece independently. The key is that these experts are not given a strict set of criteria to follow but instead rely on their intrinsic understanding and experience within the domain to judge the creativity of the work. This approach acknowledges the subjective nature of creativity, which can vary significantly across different fields and cultural contexts. This subjectivity but heavy reliance on expertise in the field comes directly as a response to earlier more imperative tests that were used to measure creativity that were criticized for not being able to identify originality and value appropriately.

The strength of CAT is in the collective judgment of these experts. By aggregating the assessments of multiple experts, the technique minimizes individual biases and idiosyncrasies, leading to a more reliable and valid measure of creativity. The level of agreement among raters (also known as inter-rater reliability) is an indicator of the robustness of the assessment. Typically, a high level of agreement among expert raters is seen as a validation of the technique's effectiveness in measuring creativity accurately. You have probably arrived to think that a lot of awards that are given to creative fields are judged utilizing a similar format, from the Oscars to the Game Developers Choice awards, a panel of experts or prominent figures in the field are collectively rendering a judgment as a measurement of creativity.

Simplicity and scalability is one of the primary advantages of CAT is its flexibility. It can be applied to a wide range of creative outputs, from written stories and scientific theories to artworks and business strategies. This versatility makes it a valuable tool in diverse fields, whether in educational settings, research, or industry. Moreover, because it doesn't rely on a predetermined set of criteria, CAT can adapt to changes and trends within a creative domain, maintaining its relevance and effectiveness over time.

However, despite its strengths, CAT is not without its challenges and limitations. Finding and recruiting experts who are willing and able to participate in the research can be difficult and time-consuming. There is also a risk that experts also hold personal biases or preferences that may influence their decisions. Furthermore, although the variability of the CAT is a strength, it also means that the method lacks the standardized standards found in more objective testing methodologies, which may complicate comparisons across subjects or projects.

The CAT is a unique and powerful method for measuring creativity. Its reliance on the subjective judgment of domain-specific experts allows it to capture the nuanced and often elusive nature of creative quality. Its flexibility allows it to be utilized in various applications and industries. We will discuss in more detail how it can be used within an organizational structure and in the games industry in Chapter 4 on innovation.

No matter the technique we use to measure creativity, the one clear thing that binds them all together is that we need to find ways to be able to identify originality, being able to measure the degree of how original it is and then evaluate how fitting it is to the context we have at hand.

From originality to value

In this chapter, we covered different ways we can arrive at originality, but at its core, it's practicing a form of creative sobriety, self-reflection, that enables us to reach into our journey of self-discovery and then apply divergent thinking to the task at hand to create hierarchies of connections between elements within ourselves. By practicing creative sobriety, we become aware of how those connections came to be and we work to ensure that the statistical likelihood of those connections is as extremely rare as possible.

Once we have an original idea generated, we need to be able to evaluate how original is that idea really, and we explored several methods to measure creativity in this chapter. In the upcoming chapters on innovation and the creative process, we will explore how once we know that we have an original idea in our hands, we can evaluate whether it's an appropriate fit to the context within which we operate.

Further Reading

Amabile, T.M. (1988). A model of creativity and innovation in organizations. *Research in Organizational Behavior*, 10(1), 123–167.

Amabile, T.M., & Hennessey, B.A. (1999). Consensual assessment. *Encyclopedia of Creativity*, 1, 347–359.

Buzan, T., & Buzan, B. (2006). *The Mind Map Book*. Pearson Education.

Cleese, J. (1991). "A Lecture on Creativity."

Duff, J.F. (1926). Genetic studies of genius. Vol. I. Mental and physical traits of a thousand gifted children. *The Eugenics Review*, 18(1), 45–47.

Frontiers. (2014). Is there an inverted-U relationship between creativity and psychopathology? [online]. Frontiers. [Viewed 25 March 2024]. https://www.frontiersin.org/journals/psychology/articles/10.3389/fpsyg.2014.00750/full

Guilford, J.P. (1956). The structure of intellect. *Psychological bulletin*, 53(4), 267.

Jung, R.E., Mead, B.S., Carrasco, J., & Flores, R.A. (2013). The structure of creative cognition in the human brain. *Frontiers in Human Neuroscience*, 7, 330.

MacKinnon, D. (1964). The creative personality. Alex Osborn Creative Studies Collection. Archives & Special Collections Department, E. H. Butler Library, SUNY Buffalo State. https://digitalcommons.buffalostate.edu/cs-speakers/1

Mednick, S. (1962). The associative basis of the creative process. *Psychological Review*, 69(3), 220.

Oltețeanu, A. (2016). Towards Using Cognitive Word Associates to Create Functional Remote Associates Test Problems. 2016 *12th International Conference on Signal-Image Technology & Internet-Based Systems (SITIS)*, Naples, Italy 612–617.

Simonton, D.K. (2014). More method in the mad-genius controversy: a historiometric study of 204 historic creators. *Psychology of Aesthetics, Creativity, and the Arts*, 8, 53–61. doi: 10.1037/a0035367

Torrance, E.P. (1966). Torrance tests of creative thinking. *norms technical manual research edition—verbal tests, forms A and B—figural tests, forms A and B. Princeton: Personnel Pres. Inc.*

Chapter 4
Innovation

> You're mad, bonkers, completely off your head. But I'll tell you a secret. All the best people are.
>
> —Lewis Carroll

Innovation and creativity are without a doubt interlaced concepts, but they are not one and the same.

As we have discussed so far, creativity is the mental, personal, and social process involving the generation of new ideas or concepts, or new associations between existing ideas or concepts that are original and of value. It's an intrinsic ability that we all have that can be applied to any domain of life, from the arts to everyday problem-solving. Creativity is about originality and the ability to perceive the world in novel ways, to make connections between seemingly unrelated phenomena, and to generate solutions to problems that we perceive or that we impose upon ourselves. Creativity involves acting on these ideas, and the outcome doesn't necessarily need to benefit an organization; the value of creativity lies in the potential of the creative thought itself, regardless of its practical application. Within creativity, one can create art for art's sake or improvise music on the spot to convey their motions, merely to express how the world touches us.

DOI: 10.1201/9781003261834-4

Defining innovation

Innovation is a subset within creativity; it is one that focuses on the implementation or actualization of creative ideas to produce a tangible new product, service, process, or improvement within an organization. It's about applying creative outputs to bring about change or introduce newness to a particular field or market. Innovation involves a series of steps that include idea development, prototyping, testing, and refining. It is not just production ideas that are not only original but also the practical execution of those thoughts, leading to something that can be introduced into the market or society, and that adds value. If by practicing creative sobriety we know how we can better arrive at originality, then studying innovation enables evaluating how we can arrive at a value context of usefulness and practicality.

The starting point of innovation would be applying the creative process to generate new ideas, and we will dive into defining the creative process and different ideation methodologies in Chapter 5. Though all innovation starts with creative ideas, not all creative ideas lead to innovation. Creativity is necessary but not sufficient for innovation. Innovation requires the realization of the potential of those creative ideas.

Creativity is a domain-agnostic trait that individuals or groups can exhibit in any area of expertise or domain of knowledge, whereas innovation is more associated with technical, organizational, or business contexts. Innovation is more directly tied to goals like increasing competitiveness, efficiency, or customer/user/player satisfaction. Creativity produces the raw material that goes through the processes of innovation that shape that material into a usable form.

In many ways, if creativity is to generate ideas that are both original and valuable, then the quest for innovation is to determine the value of those ideas and bring them to fruition.

The pace of technical innovation

Technological innovation is advancing and accelerating at a pace that is unprecedented in human history. A growth rate that is much more exponential than it is linear, largely due to a complex interplay of various factors, each contributing to the speed at which technology evolves and reshapes our world.

In 1965, American Engineer Gordon Moore observed that the number of transistors on a microchip doubles approximately every two years, while the cost of computers is halved. This trend—also known as Moore's law—has led to an exponential increase in computational capabilities, enabling devices to become more powerful, smaller, and cheaper at an increasingly rapid pace. As a result, individuals and organizations have been empowered to innovate on an increasingly advanced technological canvas, leading to faster cycles of innovation and iteration across many fields than any other time in human history as well.

Couple that with digital connectivity, and you would get a pace of innovation that has been even further compounded. The internet and related technology have created a network effect, as it connected all of us, which means that every one of us is adding value and capabilities to this global innovation effort. Ideas, research, and innovations can now be shared instantly across the world, which allows for instant collaboration and development that is not bound by a physical location. We are daily engaging in a global brainstorm that has significantly sped up the iteration of ideas, problem-solving, and a much much quicker pace of technological advancement. It also allows for the convergence of different disciplines, as one breakthrough in one area will have immediate and profound implications for others. It's analogous inspiration that the generalists have applied to a massive scale of our entire planet. Perhaps the most recent cross-national response to the COVID-19 global pandemic and the speed in which a vaccine was developed is a testament to the pace of accelerated innovation that takes place around the world at the same time.

This pace is also fueled by an unprecedented level of investment in research and development. Private enterprises and public institutions alike are pouring resources into discovering and developing new technologies that are innovating on other inventions that are presented to the world at a rapid pace. R&D is not just about being first to market but also about survival, as companies that fail to keep up and innovate will risk obsolescence. Fierce competition and substantial financial backing significantly shorten the innovation cycle which is contributing to an even faster pace of technological advancement.

As a result, our societies have adapted a culture that values innovation and entrepreneurship, as individuals and organizations are encouraged to take risks and disrupt established norms constantly. Start-ups and tech companies adapt agile methodologies that embrace change and risk-taking as part of their development cycles, to continue pushing the boundaries often resulting in disruption of established industries with new innovative solutions. This culture even democratizes the pace of cultural change, with grassroots innovation coming out of garages and small labs just as much as it's coming out of large corporate R&D departments.

On the flip side, this fast pace can lead to innovations outstripping the ability of regulations and societal norms to adapt, creating gaps where technology moves faster than ethical guidelines can be established, which leads to societal disruptions from job displacement, security, and privacy issues to various other ethical considerations.

As we approach the limits of how small semiconductor components can be made, the continuation of Moore's law as we know it is in question, the pace of innovation due to the other factors is in full swing and is unlikely to slow down. History has shown that often when one avenue slows, alternative paths of innovation are discovered. The slowing of semiconductor miniaturization has led to increased interest in areas like quantum and neuromorphic computing. The pace of technical innovation is not just a characteristic of development, but it's a phenomenon that is driven by a combination of technological, economic, cultural, and societal factors. It's a pace that's reshaping industries, economies, and lifestyles at a never-before-seen rate in human history. That offers incredible opportunities while also posing significant challenges. The future will likely be marked by continued acceleration in innovation and the ability to adapt and manage that pace will play a critical role in any industry's success, and ours is no different.

I remember a time in the early 1990s, when the video games industry was moving away from cartridges to embrace CDs with the release of the Sony PlayStation and Sega CD making that shift. That was a move that significantly increased storage capacity from a few megabytes to 650–700 MBs, allowing for much more complex games with better graphics and audio. We could have full motion video FMVs, sweeping soundtracks, and even voice-over dialogue that used to take a lot more space than developers could afford on a cartridge. It was also a lot cheaper to manufacture, transport, and became the industry standard in no time. It wasn't long before DVDs offered a substantial increase in storage up to 8.5 GB, enabling even more sophisticated games with much higher quality video and audio content. Then Sony once again adopted new technology by including a Blu-ray player for their PlayStation 3 release, which further increased storage to 50 GB. This not only became the optimum way for storage for gaming consoles but also for all other high-definition (HD) video in the broader media market at large.

As you can see from just the storage medium example, the video game industry has always been profoundly impacted by the rapid pace of technical innovation, which has reshaped everything around our industry and that's bound to continue to happen. However, we have also seen that because the gaming industry adopted certain technologies—or in some cases pioneered it—then that technology ended up being used outside of the industry in other fields. There is symbiotic relationship between the games industry and technology that is constantly propelling both forward. That can manifest along the following vectors:

Game development and design

This vector revolves around the different methods around how we develop and design games within the industry. It includes the variety of technology hardware and software that is likely to drive our industry forward and has been for the recent years of the time of writing this.

- **Advanced Graphics and Processing Power:** As hardware continues to evolve, games can now offer more realistic graphics, complex simulations, and immersive experiences. High-fidelity graphics, realistic physics, and sophisticated AI make virtual worlds more engaging and lifelike. Developers can create expansive, detailed game environments that were previously impossible and enable them to push the boundaries of creativity and storytelling. For our generation of gamers, where we started out with low fidelity graphics, there's a section of the fan base that will seek more immersive and realistic experiences, which require more powerful proces-sors, advanced graphics cards, high-resolution displays, and faster access to memory. This demand will, in turn, spur advancement in the hardware technology sector. The demand for high-fidelity graph-ics has pushed the development of more powerful graphics cards which in turn found application in other fields like scientific research and cryptocurrency mining. The same happened in the CPU tech-nology, cooling systems, and even display technologies like OLED and high refresh rate monitors.

- **Emerging Technologies:** Technologies like virtual reality (VR), augmented reality (AR), and mixed reality (MR) are presenting new ways to experience gameplay beyond what we've done before through monitors. VR immerses players in 3D worlds, providing a sense of presence that traditional games can't match. AR games blend digital content with the real world, opening up endless pos-sibilities for gameplay tied to physical locations and movements. Games provide a compelling use case for immersive technologies which in turn pushes for their development and refinement making them more viable for other applications, which in turn participate in speeding up their pace of innovation. Games like *Beat Saber* for VR and *Pokémon Go* for AR have not only demonstrated the mass-mar-ket appeal of these technologies but have also encouraged many companies to invest in research and development in those areas. As these technologies improve within gaming, they become more viable and effective for other applications, thereby accelerating their overall pace of innovation and adoption in fields such as education, training, and real estate.

- **Procedural Generation and AI:** As the scope of the games we develop becomes larger, further solutions are needed to allow for the creation of vast and dynamic worlds with minimal human input. Games also grew to become a complex network of systems that interact with each other and allow for making each player's experi-ence unique, which led to lots of innovation in procedural genera-tion but also of AI. AI improvements make non-player characters (NPCs) more realistic and responsive, enhancing immersion and gameplay complexity. Games are profoundly complex pieces of soft-ware. Developing a modern game involves solving so many difficult problems in graphics rendering, physics simulation, artificial intelligence, networking, and more. I am deliberately leaving out artistic and design problems here to keep the focus on the technological innovation aspect of this chapter. Solving these problems often requires a lot of innovative software solutions. For instance, game AI has driven advancements in pathfinding algorithms and behavior simulation. Real-time graphics rendering in games pushes the development of more efficient, realistic rendering techniques, which are then used in other industries like film and virtual prototyping.

Distribution and access

Technology plays a huge factor in how we get the games that we play. The past where a consumer would simply head to their local supermarket or toy store to purchase a boxed copy of a game while still a viable method is becoming only one of the ways we can gain access to games. That doesn't only affect consumer behavior but also the way we make games as well. Several technological innovations have changed the lay of the land over the past few years and will likely continue to do so in the near future as well.

- **Digital Distribution:** The rise of digital storefronts has revolutionized game distribution. Players can now purchase and download games from anywhere, often at lower costs and with more convenience than physical copies. This shift has also lowered barriers for indie developers, who can now reach global audiences without the need for physical distribution deals. It also meant that we could instantly deliver content to the players even long after they've purchased the game, which in turn changed the way we schedule development times for games, giving us more time to make the games, more time to service them, and methods of keeping players engaged and happy for years after the game's initial release.
- **Cloud Gaming and Streaming:** Cloud gaming services allow games to be streamed directly to devices, bypassing the need for powerful hardware. This innovation democratizes access to high-end games since players with even the most modest systems can enjoy the latest titles. Several companies such as Sony, Microsoft, and even for

a little while, Google embraced the undeniable convince of this technology. While the infrastructure and prevalence of ultra high speed and low latency internet are not there yet, it's a question of when and if this technology will become available, and we see companies already preparing for that—in my opinion—inevitable future. Additionally, streaming platforms like Twitch have created communities around gaming, changing how games are marketed and enjoyed. You can now play games with others regardless of where you are, you can have audiences of people watching you play, and as cloud gaming evolves, you can also have a future where you play directly with that audience.

- **Mobile Gaming:** The proliferation of smartphones has opened a massive market for mobile games. With every one of us almost carrying one of these devices on our person, suddenly everyone now has a gaming console in their pockets, and lots of games come out with smartphone compatibility in mind. These games range from more casual bite sized games that you can enjoy for a few minutes while waiting for the bus to sophisticated titles that are similar to—or are—traditional console and PC games in complexity and narrative. Mobile gaming has expanded the audience for games, bringing in demographics that traditionally might not consider themselves gamers. A lot of modern mobile games have cross compatibility and cross-play with their traditional counterparts, meaning that players on different systems can now play together. Changing the way we play games together, and bringing in more and more people to the industry but also how we approach the design and structure of those games as we make them.

Player experience and community

Technology has also radically advanced the way we connect with each other and the creation of the games itself. There used to be a time when gaming machines were in a physical space like the arcades where we used to gather to play together and connect. Not only with other players but also with how games are made themselves. Technological innovation has propelled us forward.

- **Online Multiplayer and Connectivity:** The internet has turned the entire world into a giant arcade as online multiplayer games allow people to play together or against each other from anywhere in the globe. When they're playing against each other, some of them have advanced their skill to such a point that it's a sight to behold, and the internet allowed for the masses to turn it into spectator events known as eSports, where players compete professionally, and massive online communities form around favorite games, teams, players, and personalities. The rise of Massive Multiplayer Online Games (MMOs) like *World of Warcraft* required robust online infrastructures, pushing forward the development of better networking technologies and servers. This need for connectivity laid the groundwork for the aforementioned cloud gaming platforms and technologies. As we are social creatures, gaming has allowed us to connect more than others before. This shift is not just limited to gaming; it potentially influences how other media might be streamed and consumed in the future.
- **Modding and User-Generated Content:** Many developers now support modding communities, players that modify the games they like through a variety of tools, some of them provided by the developers themselves, recognizing that they can significantly extend a game's lifespan and appeal. User-generated content ranges from new game levels and items to complete overhauls that can transform the game entirely. The gaming community is known for its enthusiastic embrace of technology and innovation. Gamers are not just consumers but active participants, modding games, and creating content. This culture fosters an environment of innovation, with community members often pushing technology to its limits, discovering new uses, and creating tools and modifications that feed back into the industry. Many game developers started as modders, and the innovations they create often find their way into mainstream gaming and other technology sectors. As developers, we are constantly observing in admiration the creativity and innovation that come out of the modding communities and view it as yet another source of inspiration for the experiences we create. The innovation cycle connects the developers with the players even on a creation level.

Economic and industry impacts

The gaming industry is hugely profitable, we are bigger in terms of revenue than movies, music, books, and television combined. This creates significant economic incentives for technological innovation. Companies invest heavily in research and development to gain an edge in a very competitive and lucrative market. The potential rewards for creating a hit game with innovative technology are substantial, which drives a continual push for better, more advanced technology.

- **Indie Game Boom:** Technological advancements and digital distribution have lowered the barriers to game development and publishing. This shift has led to an indie game boom, with small teams and even solo developers creating hit games. These indie titles often push the boundaries of traditional gameplay and narrative, driving innovation within the industry. The indie game space is a thriving space with gameplay innovation at its core, with small teams across the world experimenting with different ways to craft experiences and tell stories. The small size of the teams and budgets means that we're getting games from places where we didn't get games before, which is enriching the output of our medium and allowing us access to ideas as inspiration that we didn't have access to before without the gate keeping of the past. Some of those games grow popular to the point that they become franchises of their own, growing companies, creating jobs and in some areas, even boosting the economy.
- **Monetization Models:** The technology also enables diverse monetization strategies, from traditional sales to free-to-play models supported by microtransactions. Subscription models, season passes, and in-game purchases have become common, influencing how games are designed and consumed.
- **Global Reach:** Our industry is more global than ever, with games developed and played worldwide, with game makers learning their crafts coming in from anywhere on earth, with games-enabled devices that are more accessible than ever. Gaming is a huge international phenomenon with far reach. This global reach influences the cultural content of games, marketing strategies, and the recognition of gaming as a significant cultural and economic force.

Governments are investing in games and providing incentives for gaming companies to come and open shop within their borders. Game makers are being knighted and honored by Kings and presidents. It's undoubtedly the economic impact that a successful gaming company will have on a micro and macro economy of a region. It's a much sought-after growth segment in any country's growth and development plan.

The rapid pace of technical innovation has fundamentally transformed the video game industry, and vice versa! It has led to more sophisticated and diverse games, changed how games are distributed and played, and expanded the industry's economic and cultural impact. And at the same time, the video games industry has significantly contributed to how people interact with computers and pushed innovation on so many different industries outside of entertainment. As technology continues to evolve, the video game industry is likely to see further significant changes, offering new opportunities and challenges for developers, players, and the industry as a whole. The gaming industry continues to evolve, it will no doubt push the innovation pace forward on the industries and sectors it influences as a result as well.

The technology developed for gaming doesn't stay confined to the industry. Graphics processors designed for games are used in movie production and medical imaging. Game development tools and engines are used to create simulations and training applications. The cloud infrastructure built for online gaming is used for a wide variety of cloud-based applications. In this way, the gaming industry not only benefits from broader technological advancements but also contributes back to it, influencing the pace of innovation across multiple sectors.

Disruptive technology

Every now and then, there are technologies that are significant enough to sweep away habits or systems and completely replace them with a new way of operating, whether it's for consumers, industries, or businesses. Those technologies will possess qualities that are so superior to the current status quo that a change is inevitable. Disruptive technologies are not just an evolutionary step to making things better, they are revolutionary ideas that change the nature of production and societal adaptation.

Disruptive technologies often enter the market at a lower performance than their prevailing counterparts of products and services, but they have features that are generally novel and appeal to a fringe customer value that improves over time until they achieve the performance levels that the mainstream demands all while retaining the advantages that drove their early adoption. This trajectory allows them to eventually overtake and even displace established products and services.

Computers, for example, were giant mainframes and minicomputers that were large-scale machines that were beyond the affordability of individuals. They were mostly machines that are available for institutes and large corporations due to their size and expensive cost. The introduction of the personal computer democratized computing and made it accessible and affordable to homes and small businesses. This was a monumental change in how we live and how we work. The PC revolutionized industries and laid the groundwork for the Information Age.

Compounded on that, the Internet was yet another pivotal disruption. Just like computing it used to be a tool that only academics, researchers or military organizations used. The widespread distribution of PCs around the world paved the way for a global network that became a platform that has reshaped—and continues to reshape—communication, commerce and knowledge dissemination. It flipped traditional business models head over heels, and created new ones in their place. The internet's impact extends beyond economic measures; it's a monumental moment in human history. It has changed how societies communicate, learn, and entertain themselves forever.

In a very similar fashion, the now widespread distribution of smartphones is yet another distributive technology that swept through our lives and changed it forever. They've managed to transcend their primary function as portable telephones to become central hubs for personal computing, media, navigation, social interactions, and so much more. They have replaced cameras, maps, and numerous other everyday tools, altering the way people interact with the world and with each other. The smartphone's ubiquity and wide range of applications spawned entire industries and changed the landscape for so many others and many more to come.

Some disruptive technologies come out of necessity. Renewable energy technologies like solar panels and wind turbines are much needed disruptive forces in the energy sectors to shift the focus from fossil fuels to sustainable alternatives. It's a shift that fundamentally changes the very way energy is produced, distributed, and consumed. It involves rethinking infrastructure, regulations, consumer behavior and often ways of operating for nations and geopolitical nations. It's a profound disruption that offers a path to mitigate climate change and reshape dynamics between countries forever.

Being on the lookout for disruptive innovation is an existential topic for businesses and of significant implications for individuals. For businesses, ignoring or dismissing the potential of an innovation can be perilous. History is filled with examples of industry titans who failed to adapt to the disruptive change that is sweeping their market, and consequently faced decline or obsolescence. Kodak was once the dominant force of the photography sector, top seller of both cameras, films and development centers. The R&D division of the company actually had developed digital photography cameras, but that strategy was refused by the leadership of the time fearing that they'd throw away the revenue they were making off of selling film cartridges for cameras and the revenue that their development labs were bringing in. Due to the convenience of digital photography, Kodak eventually filed for Chapter 11 bankruptcy in 2012 and emerged afterwards as a new company that shed all of its historical legacy fully embracing digital photography at the core of its modern business. Having missed the boat however, it is now a much smaller player in that market.

If we think about it, video games in themselves are disruptive technology as the concept of interactive entertainment is revolutionary in its own right. The more people were exposed to it, the more prevalent and captivated it was as a form of entertainment. Similar to computing, early video game machines were large in size and unaffordable to most people; people either played video games in their early days in universities and academic institutes, which were part of the few places where you can even find a computer or later in the 1970s on arcade machines either in dedicated establishments or in your local pizza place. A major disruption happened to the industry when home consoles were introduced and that fundamentally changed the way we consume video games, slowly the arcade business shrank and video games being played on personal computing devices, smartphones or home consoles became the prominent way to consume video games.

Disruptive technologies and recognizing them is a major part of the modern day marketplace and jobs, even more so in our industry. Some innovations soar while others falter could be due to technical shortcomings, regulatory hurdles, or simply because they fail to gain sufficient market traction. There's an element of recognizing a time and a place for the technology to truly take off, but there are other considerations that we take into account as well, especially on the social and ethical dimensions. Disruptive technologies can lead to significant societal shifts, not all of which are positive, and should therefore be handled with care and a sense of responsibility.

Types of innovation

Whenever I presented my thoughts on the topic of creativity and originality in conference, there were usually many questions on my thoughts on creativity in video games and whether I agreed—I didn't—that the industry is "No longer creative", attendees mostly refer to recent releases in their favored gaming franchise and how that is not "innovating anymore". In fact, in many companies I've worked in as well, I would occasionally encounter discussions with designers and creatives who feel that there isn't a sufficient push for innovation in our industry lately.

Those mixed feelings usually come from two major factors, either confusing the different types of innovation or the fact that a lot of companies are suffering from the innovator's dilemma. We'll go through both, starting out with detailing the different types of innovation. Innovation can come in one of two types, either radical innovation or incremental.

Radical innovation

This is a type of innovation that is transformative at its core, changing the landscape entirely of whatever space they come up in. It's a type of leap that redefines industries, creates new markets and alters the way we interact with the medium, sector or even the world around us after. It's a groundbreaking shift in innovation that introduces unprecedented levels of novelty and change.

Radical innovation appears to have come out of nowhere—a breakthrough at such a level of novelty that introduces things that were previously unimaginable. Entirely new concepts redefine the parameters of what's possible. A lot of disruptive technologies that we discussed before can fall within the scope of radical innovation.

Radical innovation gets its name from how much of a radical departure it is from the previous known solutions or status quo of its landscape before its appearance. Often hailed as a monumental achievement in human creativity, ingenuity, and prowess, they're often standout moments in history. They're so rare and far in between that they're studied and observed for their everlasting impact as it's profound and extensive. The idea of the core of radical innovation is difficult to trace to a source of inspiration, and that's the heart of where it's rare, because it's difficult to obtain and reproduce. To arrive at an idea that leads to radical innovation, the idea would most probably come out of accidental creativity that we discussed in Chapter 1 or from incremental innovation over a gradual period of time (more on that later).

Street Fighter II creating the combo systems, and Nishikado inventing difficulty curves are two examples of radical innovation in video games. They embody a lot of the things that distinguish radical innovation: the origin is through accidental innovation, the source of inspiration is the accident itself, and upon introduction of the innovation, it changes the landscape completely, disrupts current standards, and replaces them with new ones.

For radical innovation to emerge, it requires a culture that encourages creativity, in all of its forms, especially accidental creativity, driven through experimentation and a tolerance of failure. It's a space that facilitates spaces for idea generation and repeated testing, and is willing to provide the resources and support needed to develop and refine those ideas, knowing that they may never materialize into a final output. Open innovation models that allow firms to look beyond their boundaries for ideas and technologies is an example of environments that can provide access to divergent thinking and potential breakthroughs. The pursuit of such innovation requires long-term commitment that looks beyond current market needs, it seeks to reinvent the future and would require an investment in research and development that is prepared for the long haul. Companies that succeed in achieving this aren't only the ones that employ highly creative individuals but also ones that are patient and resilient, ready to navigate the lengthy and uncertain path towards making a radical idea a reality.

While radical innovation is without a doubt the most desirable, given how much novelty and impact it can generate, it's the most difficult and hard-to-forecast type of innovation. It's harder to predict and even harder to make it a reality once it does occur. The other type of creativity, however, is the one that we're probably a lot more accustomed to.

Incremental innovation

Incremental innovation is the process of making small-scale improvements and refinements to existing products, services, or processes. Unlike radical innovations that appear to come out of nowhere and create significant disruptions to the sector they're in, often redefining it, incremental innovation focuses on enhancing and optimizing what already exists. It's a continuous, iterative process that gradually improves design, function, value, efficiency, productivity, quality, competitiveness, or performance.

Incremental innovation is defined by its subtlety and persistence. It focuses on continuous improvements, making minor changes that, when accumulated over time, can lead to significant improvements and perceived radical innovation. This type of innovation is typically less risky than radical innovation since it requires less investment. However, it requires a consistent commitment to refining and improving products or services, which can be a challenge in itself. In most design processes including game design, incremental innovation is part of the design process with continuous testing and iteration, and it is what leads to creating better games (Figure 4.1).

Video game developers often release updates, patches, and sequels that build upon the original game's foundation; they would introduce new features, fix bugs, or enhance graphics or user interfaces. Incremental innovation is also evident in the development of game controllers. From the simple joystick of the early Atari consoles to today's

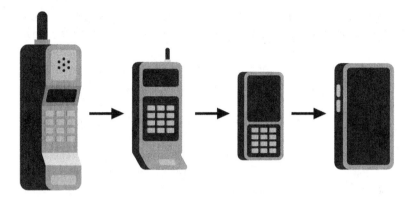

Evolution of Mobile Phones

Figure 4.1 Incremental innovation that lead to evolution of mobile phones.

complex controllers with multiple buttons, triggers, and motion sensors, each generation of controllers has built upon the last, refining the design and adding new features to enhance the gaming experience. The introduction of haptic feedback, for instance, was an incremental innovation that provided a new layer of immersion by allowing players to feel vibrations or movements in response to in-game actions.

It's important to note that incremental innovation is not just about adding more features or making things bigger. It's also about simplification and removal. Sometimes, making a product or service better means taking away what is unnecessary, streamlining processes, or making it more accessible and user-friendly. In gaming, this might mean simplifying a cluttered user interface, improving the intuitiveness of controls, or reducing the complexity of a game to appeal to a broader audience.

I remember a time in the early 1990s following the release of *DOOM* by Id Software, in which every game that was a first person shooter was called a *DOOM* clone. In fact, back in that era, that was the name of the genre, as the term FPS wasn't widely used yet.

Nowadays it's a lot more ubiquitous, and if I ask you to think of a game like *Fallout 4*, would you call that a *Doom* clone? Probably not. Since the release of *Doom* and other FPS games of its time, there has been continuous refinement and incremental innovation on the mechanics, that it transcended its genre to other genres, it became an outstanding mechanic that is utilized across the board, even modern FPS games utilizes camera angles, graphics and techniques that have nothing to do with the FPS games of that early era. When incremental innovation is applied over a long period of time it leads to experiences that are *Radically* different, though they are standing on the shoulders of giants.

Most people think of radical innovation when they think of innovation within their medium; the truth, however, is that it's so rare for it to occur that people often confuse it with incremental innovation because they think of the final result without the knowledge of all the increments and iterations that happened over a period of time for that final result to come to pass.

One of the best examples of incremental innovations leading to radical innovation in video games—also one of my all-time favorites—is *Tetris*, Alexey Pajitnov was working for the computer center of the soviet academy of sciences as a speech recognition researcher. This allowed him access to computers that many didn't at the time while he was initially tasked with testing the capabilities of the hardware he started developing several puzzle games on the institute's computer the Electronika 60 (Figure 4.2).

In 1984, Paijitnov was trying to recreate one of his favorite childhood puzzle games that featured pentominoes. The game used to have 18 different plastic pieces that the kids could arrange into any shape they wanted. He imagined a game where those pieces would fall down, and the player would turn to fill rows. Eventually, he thought that the game would be needlessly complicated with twelve different shape variations, so he scaled the concept down to tetrominoes, of which there are seven variants only. The name was then called *Tetris* as a combination of "Tetra" which means four and Paijitnov's favorite sport, Tennis.

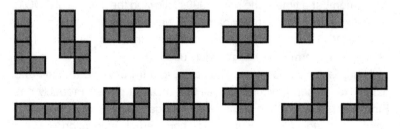

Figure 4.2 Pentominoes.

Alexy drew from an inspiration coming in from his childhood—this might sound familiar—then he made incremental adjustments to it until he arrived at one of the most celebrated and best selling games of all time, that got to us out of nowhere from the Soviet Union, from a developer that seemingly was making his first game. The radical innovation of Tetris came from a developer who after making several other puzzle games, iterated on an idea until it incrementally became Tetris.

The innovator's dilemma

The Innovator's Dilemma is a concept first introduced by Harvard Business School professor Clayton M. Christensen in his 1997 book of the same name. It describes the challenging situation that companies face when they must choose between holding onto an existing market by doing what they have always done or capturing new markets by embracing new technologies or strategies. The dilemma arises because the very practices that lead to a company's success in established markets can actually become obstacles in the face of technological change and market evolution.

The Kodak story that we described earlier is a classic Innovator's Dilemma. How an established company responds to disruptive technologies determines their survival. Disruptive technologies are typically cheaper, simpler, smaller, and, frequently, more convenient to use. They come from smaller companies or individuals with everything to gain and nothing to lose and open up new markets and potential for growth but often at lower profit margins at the beginning. Established companies are usually focused on improving their products and services for their most demanding (and most profitable) customers. As a result, they tend to overlook the disruptive technologies that don't initially meet the needs of their main customer base or that could erode their profitability, like when Kodak ignored digital cameras as they didn't serve their film consumer base. Over time, these disruptive technologies improve, begin to invade the mainstream market, and ultimately displace established products and firms, sometimes—like with Kodak—driving them out of business.

Many companies keep falling into the Innovator's Dilemma for several reasons. First, they prioritize customer-driven innovation. While usually a sound strategy, this can lead to overlooking disruptive technologies that current customers don't want or see the need for. Second, established companies often focus on maximizing their return on investment. Investing in disruptive technologies that initially have lower profit margins seems unattractive compared to improving existing, higher-margin products. Third, the organizational culture and processes in successful companies are geared toward doing what they already do well, not toward exploring uncertain, new terrain. This can stifle innovation and prevent companies from venturing into new markets with different requirements.

Zynga and other social gaming giants saw huge success on social media platforms such as Facebook; they amassed large player bases and generated a lot of revenue in the early 2000s. There were hundreds of millions of players playing Farmville as it took the world by storm. The rise of smartphones and connection to Facebook created an Innovator's Dilemma for the company, which focused on their core audience on web-based platforms and couldn't anticipate and keep up with the rise of smartphone games, and other intrants that came with it such as King and Supercel. By the time Zynga managed to catch up on portable platforms, they were no longer the dominant force that they were during the social gaming era.

Another example is the shift from physical to digital distribution of games. Many established companies were heavily invested in the physical distribution of games and were hesitant to shift towards digital distribution, fearing it would cannibalize their existing sales. However, as digital platforms like Steam, Xbox Live, and the PlayStation Network grew, they drastically changed how people purchased and played games. Companies that didn't adapt quickly enough found themselves at a significant disadvantage.

So, how do companies get out of the Innovator's Dilemma? Escaping this dilemma requires strategic, organizational, and cultural shifts within the company. The escape plan is achievable by applying the following eight steps:

1. Companies need to adopt a dual strategy. They must continue to innovate at the sustaining level to support their current customers and markets while also investing in disruptive technologies that

have the potential to create new markets. This dual approach can be challenging to manage because it involves different processes, values, and profit models, but it's crucial for long-term survival and growth.

2. Companies should foster a culture of innovation that encourages taking risks and exploring potentially disruptive technologies. This involves not just accepting failure but embracing it as a learning opportunity. Companies need to create separate teams or divisions tasked with exploring new technologies and markets. These teams should have the autonomy to pursue innovative ideas without the constraints of the core business's processes and profit expectations.

3. Companies should engage in continuous market and technology horizon scanning. They need to be aware of emerging trends, technologies, and potential disruptors. This requires not just looking at current competitors but also at companies in other sectors that could potentially enter and disrupt the market.

4. Companies should develop a customer base in new markets early, even if these markets are small and initially less profitable. By establishing a foothold in new markets, companies can learn and adapt as the market grows and changes. This can provide them with a significant advantage as the market matures and becomes more profitable.

5. Companies should consider strategic partnerships or acquisitions with firms that are developing disruptive technologies. This can provide them with valuable expertise and capabilities that they might lack internally. It can also help them enter new markets more quickly and effectively.

6. The leadership team should clearly understand and support the need for investment in disruptive technologies. They need to be prepared to defend these investments to stakeholders, particularly when the short-term return might not be immediately evident.

7. Companies should encourage experimentation and be willing to pivot based on what they learn. This might mean abandoning or radically changing a project if it's not working or if market conditions change. Flexibility and adaptability are key.

8. Companies need to continuously evaluate and refine their strategies in response to changing market conditions and emerging technologies. This requires a willingness to question assumptions and to change course when necessary.

The Innovator's Dilemma is a significant challenge for established companies. The practices that have made them successful in the past can become liabilities in the face of disruptive change. Once the nature of this dilemma is understood, then strategies to address it can be formed.

The survival of companies in the face of constant change in an age of rapid technological advancement is awareness of current circumstances, flexibility to change, and fully embracing innovation as a business need just as much as it's a cultural need.

But how do companies choose which innovations to invest in? The most prominent way for idea selection based on the context of value is through the innovation funnel.

The innovation funnel

The innovation funnel is a critical concept in business and product development. It uses a funnel as a visual representation to understand the journey from idea generation to market launch. Its structured approach helps organizations manage the complex process of turning abstract ideas into successful, market-ready innovations, from a principle of getting as many ideas into one end of a funnel to getting the one that'll get the investment on the other side (Figure 4.3).

The concept of the innovation funnel has evolved over time, but its origins are often attributed to the broader work on innovation processes and models that emerged in the mid-20th century by management theorists like Peter Drucker who laid the groundwork by discussing the importance of innovation and systematic approaches to entrepreneurial strategies. Over time, the funnel model was refined by various scholars and practitioners who recognized the need for a structured yet flexible approach to manage the innovation process. The framework generally goes through several stages, and at the end of each stage, there's usually a point of evaluation or a gate meeting. Experts on the field and stakeholders are called upon—similar to what we discussed in the CAT method in Chapter 3—to review the current status, and make a decision about passing an idea through to the other stage or stopping it.

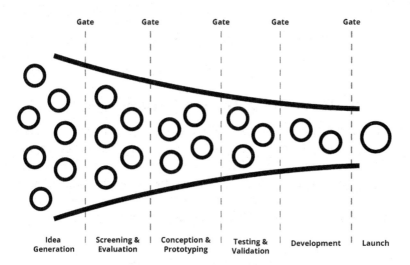

Figure 4.3 The innovation funnel.

Phase one: Idea generation

The top of the funnel is the broadest part, representing the initial stage where the quantity of ideas is valued over quality. Here, diverse and numerous ideas are encouraged through various means such as brainstorming sessions (we will discuss those in a lot more detail in Chapter 5), employee suggestions, customer feedback, open innovation platforms, and observing market trends and emerging technologies. The goal at this stage is to foster a creative environment where novel concepts can emerge without the constraints of practicality or current strategy.

Phase two: Screening and evaluation

As ideas move on to the next stage, they are scrutinized and evaluated based on various predetermined criteria (the value of the idea comes to mind here). This could include the idea's relevance to the company's strategic goals, its feasibility in terms of technology and resources, its potential market demand, its alignment with consumer needs and trends, how it aligns with the creative vision, and many more ways to determine value. This stage is crucial for narrowing down ideas to ensure that only the most valuable, promising, and aligned with company goals are carried forward.

Phase three: Conception and prototyping

In the conception phase, selected ideas are transformed into tangible prototypes or detailed plans. This involves cross-functional collaboration among teams such as R&D, design, engineering, and marketing. The development stage is characterized by its iterative nature, often involving cycles of building, testing, and refining. It usually involves small agile teams that enable quick decision-making and iteration.

Phase four: Testing and validation

This stage is critical for assessing the viability of the developed concepts. Prototypes are tested in real-world scenarios or through market research to gather feedback. This feedback is crucial for understanding the product's reception, functionality, and any issues or improvements needed.

Phase five: Development

Once an idea has passed the testing phase, it moves into implementation. This stage involves finalizing the design, ramping up production, and preparing for market launch. It's here that the logistical, financial, and operational aspects are in full swing. Supply chains are established, production processes are all set up, and marketing strategies are finalized. This is the part when it's all hands on deck, everyone is working towards the finalization and fully creating the product with all of its requirements.

Phase six: Launch

The final stage is where the innovation is introduced to the market. This involves executing the marketing plan, selling the product, and monitoring its performance. After launch, the company continues to track sales, customer feedback, and market reception to understand the product's impact and any further improvements or iterations needed. When a game company launches a new game, it monitors initial sales, player feedback, and online reviews to gauge its success and quickly address any issues or bugs.

Gates

The gates at the end of each of those phases serve as critical check-points that compartmentalize the innovation process into distinct phases. They are decision points where ideas, concepts, or projects are reviewed against specific criteria before resources are committed to move them forward. Gates are integral to a structured approach known as stage-gate or phase-gate process, which helps manage the inherent risks in developing new products or services.

The primary purpose of gates is to ensure that an organization's resources are focused on the most promising initiatives. Gates help to:

- Assess the progress of projects against their objectives and alignment with strategic goals.
- Evaluate the feasibility and potential market success of a product or service.
- Make informed decisions about whether to continue, modify, or terminate a project.
- Allocate resources efficiently, failing fast, by filtering out less viable projects early on.
- Increase the chances of innovation success by imposing standards and checkpoints.

The participants at each gate typically include a cross-functional group of stakeholders known as a steering committee. This team can comprise senior management who provide strategic oversight, project managers who represent the operational aspects of the innovation projects, technical experts who can assess the technological viability, marketing and sales professionals who bring insights into market needs and commercial potential, finance experts who evaluate the financial aspects, such as cost estimates and revenue projections. Legal advisors, especially when intellectual property or regulatory compliance is a concern and subject matter experts that have deep knowledge in the product and industry to provide input and evaluation.

The composition of this committee can vary depending on the stage of the innovation process and the specific expertise required to assess the project at that point.

Conducting gate meetings

Gate meetings are typically conducted at the end of a stage, before the project moves into the next phase of development. The process is usually formal and structured, often involving the following steps:

1. **Preparation:** Prior to the meeting, the project team prepares documentation that typically includes progress reports, results from tests or market studies, updated business cases, risk assessments, and recommendations for the next steps.
2. **Presentation:** During the gate meeting, the project team presents their findings to the steering committee, highlighting key achievements, challenges, and any changes to the initial assumptions or plans.
3. **Evaluation:** The steering committee evaluates the information against predefined criteria, which can include technical feasibility, customer acceptance, product differentiation, financial metrics, and strategic fit.
4. **Decision:** After thorough discussion and evaluation, the steering committee makes a decision on the project's future. The possible outcomes include go (proceed to the next stage), stop (stop the project), hold (delay the project pending further information or changes), or recycle (send the project back to a previous stage for additional work).
5. **Feedback:** Constructive feedback is provided to the project team, along with clear reasons for the decision and, if applicable, guidance on areas that require attention in the next stage.
6. **Documentation:** The decisions and feedback are formally documented for future reference, providing a record of the innovation process and learning points for the organization.

Gate meetings are critical for several reasons. They provide structured oversight of the innovation process, which enables better risk management by breaking down the process into manageable stages. They also enhance communication and alignment across different parts of the organization, ensuring that all relevant departments are coordinated in their efforts to develop and launch new innovations. Furthermore, gate meetings facilitate learning by capturing insights from each stage of the process, which can be applied to current and future projects.

While the innovation funnel is a valuable conceptual model for understanding the innovation process, it on the flipside presents several inherent challenges that can impede an organization's ability to effectively transform ideas into successful market offerings. These challenges are numerous, and it's important to keep an eye on them for an organization to adapt and make sure that the integrity of the process is not jeopardized.

For starters, the innovation model suggests a straightforward process where ideas are generated, screened, developed, and launched in a step-by-step fashion. However, real-world innovation is rarely so orderly. Ideas often need to cycle back for further refinement; markets change rapidly requiring shifts in strategy, and feedback at any stage can significantly alter the development path. The funnel model may oversimplify the complexity and nonlinearity of real-world innovation, which leads to processes that are inflexible and unable to respond to new information or changing circumstances.

As ideas progress through the funnel, they are continually filtered and evaluated until only a few make it to the final stages. This can lead to excessive conservatism and risk aversion. There's a tendency to favor ideas that are safe, incrementally different, or closely aligned with current business models, potentially overlooking radical or unconventional ideas that could be game-changers. Over-filtering can stifle creativity and lead to a portfolio of innovations that are too safe for the organization's own good.

There's often a tendency to under-invest in the middle stages of the funnel, particularly when it comes to developing and prototyping ideas. Moreover, securing ongoing support and resources for innovation initiatives can be challenging, especially if the potential return on investment is uncertain or if there are competing priorities within the organization. A culture that fears failure or is too focused on short-term results can discourage experimentation and the exploration of new ideas.

Measuring the success of innovations, particularly in the early stages, can be challenging. Traditional financial metrics may not capture the long-term value or potential of an innovation. Moreover, there's often a reluctance to thoroughly analyze and learn from failures, leading to missed opportunities for improvement. Developing the right metrics and fostering an environment where learning from failure is seen as valuable is a challenge but essential for continuous innovation.

An interesting improvement on the innovation funnel came from Pixar with their Braintrust approach depicted in "Creativity, Inc.", where they harvest the collective wisdom of experts to evaluate creative work, with a shared belief that quality assessment hinges on diverse, informed, and nonbinding perspectives.

At Pixar, the Braintrust assembles to provide candid feedback on films in development. The Braintrust, much like a steering committee, is composed of individuals with relevant experience and expertise, but they operate *without* the authority to enforce their recommendations. This mirrors the CAT principle where creativity is assessed not by unilateral decree but through the consensus of knowledgeable individuals. The value in both the Braintrust and the gates process lies in the dialogue and the understanding that those giving feedback are not mandating changes but advising, leaving the final decision to the project's lead. This allows for a rich exchange of ideas and preserves the creative freedom of the team responsible for the work. It's an understanding that while the expertise of the group is invaluable, it is the project team that ultimately knows the intricacies of their work and has the vision for its final form.

Any structured approach to measuring and managing innovation aims to enhance the creative output to achieve the highest value and resonance with the audience or market while minimizing the risk that is inherent to innovation. In each case, the process has to be constructive, focusing on elevating the quality of the idea or product, not critiquing it. It is an approach that seeks to distill the strongest attributes of a project while identifying and resolving its weaknesses. It's an approach to measure originality against value.

The study of innovation helps greatly in identifying the methods of isolating and enhancing the value of a given idea as an integral part of creativity. However, originality is at the core of both creativity and innovation. We've discussed in Chapter 3 the importance of creative sobriety, reflection, adding personal experiences and perspectives to arrive at originality. In this chapter, we examined how we can determine value, and in Chapter 5, we study the creative processes that help us generate ideas.

Further Reading

Ackerman, D. (2016). The Tetris effect: The Cold War battle for the world's most addictive game. Simon and Schuster.

Bok, K., Sitar, S., Graham, B. S., & Mascola, J. R. (2021). Accelerated COVID-19 vaccine development: milestones, lessons, and prospects. *Immunity*, 54(8), 1636–1651.

Catmull, E., & Wallace, A. (2014). Creativity, Inc.: Overcoming the unseen forces that stand in the way of true inspiration (The Expanded Edition). Random House.

Christensen, C.M. (1997). *The Innovator's Dilemma*. Cambridge, MA: Harvard Business School Press.

Drucker, P.F. (1992). Organizations. *Harvard Business Review*, 20(7), 281–293.

Dunphy, S.M., Herbig, P.R., & Howes, M.E. (1996). The innovation funnel. *Technological Forecasting and Social Change*, 53(3), 279–292.

Edwards-Schachter, M. (2018). The nature and variety of innovation. *International Journal of Innovation Studies*, 2(2), 65–79.

Henderstot, S., & Lapetino, T. (2017). Undisputed Street Fighter: The art and innovation behind the game-changing series. Dynamite Entertainment.

Moore, G. (1965). Moore's law. *Electronics Magazine*, 38(8), 114.

Chapter 5
The creative process

The creative process is a process of surrender, not control.

–Bruce Lee

Definition

When we spoke about inspiration earlier on in Chapter 2, we spoke about how ideas get generated through insight, inspiration, or analogous connection between different concepts that seemingly have nothing to do with each other. We went through various types of inspiration, sources of it, and how our own personal life journeys can lead to that mysterious spark that ignites an idea into existence and then on which we act to build and produce an act that stems from that idea. And since that spark is where all of our creativity starts, and given that we need that creativity to innovate and produce, is there a way for us to make that spark more predictable? Is there a process that we can follow?

The creative process is not just a methodical sequence of steps, it's organic in its nature, it's an improvised dance between the conscious and subconscious mind, where knowledge, experience, intuition, observation, imagination, and projection meet in ways that are completely unique to each person. It is a form of mental pathway that we traverse as we move from the point of encountering a problem or imposing one upon ourselves until we produce an original and appropriate solution. It is our deep engagement with our inner landscape of cognition, emotion, and understanding, influenced by so many factors,

DOI: 10.1201/9781003261834-5

including one's environment, cultural background, personal experiences, and own cognitive ability and style.

Though the creative process varies wildly from person to person due to its deeply objective nature, it is widely recognized as a fundamental mechanism through which we all express our unique perspectives and contribute to humanity's culture and knowledge. We will dive much deeper into our responsibility to humanity to create in Chapter 6.

"The essence of all beautiful art, all great art, is gratitude" – Nietzsche (1886) connects the creative process with a profound sense of appreciation and recognition of the beauty of being alive. Understanding that process involves an appreciation of the journey, not just the end result. It's the human mind's ability to transcend the ordinary and bring to the world the unprecedented.

When asking about one's creative process, people are usually inquiring in understanding where those ideas are coming from, what steps were taken, or sources of inspiration were tapped into before the vague idea was formed into something more.

"The creative mind plays with the objects it loves" – Jung (1921) sees creativity as an affectionate and playful interaction with the subjects of one's focus. So in many ways, understanding the creative process first and foremost begins with creative sobriety and understanding oneself more. The more you look into yourself, the better you can articulate your creative process.

As individual as the process is, there are shared attributes that have been observed through the ages in how we create. In this chapter, we will be exploring multiple approaches to understanding the creative process through scientific models, frameworks, and techniques.

The 4Ps of creativity

The 4Ps of creativity is a framework put together by Mel Rhodes in 1961 to dissect the creative process into four dimensions: Person, Process, Press (occasionally referred to as Place), and Product. Each 'P' represents a different aspect of creativity to bring forth a holistic view on how ideas and innovations are conceived and thereafter realized (Figure 5.1).

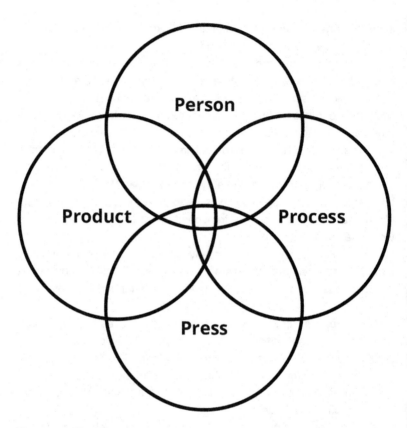

Figure 5.1 The 4Ps of creativity.

Person

This dimension is focused on the *individual* or *individuals* who are engaging in the creative act. It's the analysis of the characteristics, traits, cognitive styles, experiences, and behaviours of creative individuals to better understand what makes them more capable of producing creative work. We discussed highly creative individuals at length in Chapter 3. The study of what makes those people tick and how we measure their creativity and divergent thinking is at the heart of this dimension.

In our industry, 'Person' refers to the game designers, developers, writers, artists, musicians, and everyone else who work on the team that brings the game to life.

Process

Examines how creative ideas develop and the stages they typically pass through. In this chapter, we will discuss in detail several of these processes from Wallace's Creative process, to the genplore model, to authorship, to even some that I have put together myself.

The 'Process' of creating a video game, for example, commonly involves several stages, from conceptualization to development and testing. In the initial stages, for instance, we commonly brainstorm ideas, create thematic elements, or design characters and environments. A development phase is normally where programmers, artists, or sound engineers work together to bring the concept to life. The final stage often includes testing and refining the game to ensure a seamless and engaging player experience.

Press/place

This dimension refers to the environment or context in which the individual is creating. This includes physical surroundings, social environments, organizational culture, and societal norms. The press can significantly influence creativity by either fostering it or hindering it. Access to resources, including materials, time, and space, can affect the ability to experiment and produce creative work. Collaboration and exposure to diverse perspectives can stimulate creative ideas, while overly critical or unsupportive social environments can stifle creativity. Autonomy and freedom to explore often lead to higher levels of creative thought. By understanding the influence of the environment, strategies can be developed to create spaces that foster and enhance the creative process.

The 'Press' or environment for video games includes the technological landscape, gaming culture, market trends, or community feedback. The rapid advancement of technology has allowed for more sophisticated and immersive gaming experiences that could leverage VR hardware to create a deeply immersive experience, for example. Forums and social media allow the gaming community to provide feedback and foster discussion, which can influence the development of the game and the creative process surrounding it. Games like *Minecraft* have thrived by embracing community mods and inputs, continually evolving through the creative contributions of its players.

Product

Refers to the outcome or the result of the creative process. It's the tangible or intangible artifact that emerges from the creative process and can be an artwork, an invention, a scientific theory, a novel, or any other novel and valuable creation. The product is what typically gets evaluated to determine if something is indeed creative. It must be both novel and appropriate. Assessing the creativity of a product often involves considering its originality, relevance, elegance, and transformative impact. The creativity of the product is often measured through one or more of the methods we discussed in Chapter 4 on innovation and innovation funnels.

The 'Product' is the final game released to the public. It reflects the creativity and innovation of the development team and the impact of the environment in which it was created.

The 4Ps of creativity provide an interesting lens through which to understand how the different dimensions are interconnected and critical to each other. The person brings their traits and cognitive styles to the process that unfolds within the press, leading to the creation of a product. It's a dynamic system where each 'P' influences and is influenced by the others.

This allows us to, at a glance, understand what fosters and hinders the creative output. This knowledge can then be applied to find solutions, promote creativity in individuals and organizations, and even society at large.

By examining video games through the 4Ps of creativity framework, we can appreciate the multifaceted creative efforts that go into game development, from the individuals who envision and create the game to the processes they use, the environments that influence them, and the innovative products they bring to the gaming community. Each aspect plays a critical role in shaping the unique and captivating experiences that games provide.

The 4Ps framework, when used as an assessment tool in innovation gates (described in detail in the innovation funnel of Chapter 4), can provide a structured and holistic approach to evaluating and guiding the development of new products, services, or processes. Innovation gates are checkpoints in the innovation process where ideas are assessed and decisions are made about whether to proceed, modify, or halt the project. Using the 4Ps can help ensure a comprehensive evaluation at each gate. Here's how the framework can be applied:

- **Person:** At each innovation gate, assessing the 'Person' aspect involves evaluating the team and individuals involved in the project. This includes considering:
  o **Skills and Expertise:** Does the team have the necessary knowledge and skills to bring the innovation to life?
  o **Creativity and Diversity:** Is there a diverse range of perspectives and creative thinking styles within the team to foster innovative solutions?
  o **Motivation and Commitment:** Are the team members committed and motivated to overcome challenges and drive the project forward?

- **Process:** Here it's about assessing the methodologies and procedures used to develop the innovation. This includes evaluating:
  o **Development Stages:** Has the project successfully passed through the necessary stages of development, such as ideation, prototyping, and testing?
  o **Efficiency and Effectiveness:** Are the processes being used efficient and effective in moving the project forward?
  o **Flexibility and Adaptability:** Can the team and process adapt to new information, feedback, or changing conditions?

- **Press/Place:** Assessing the environment involves looking at the external and internal factors that might influence the innovation's success, which include:
  o **Market Trends and Needs:** Does the innovation align with current market trends and address a genuine need or business opportunity?
  o **Organizational Support:** Is there sufficient support from the organization, including resources, skills, funding, and leadership?
  o **Cultural and Regulatory Factors:** Are there cultural or regulatory considerations that might impact the development or launch of the innovation?

- **Product:** Finally, looking at the product itself, it is normally assessed on:
  - o **Originality:** Does the innovation offer something new and different from existing solutions?
  - o **Value and Relevance:** Does it provide significant value to the intended users or stakeholders?
  - o **Feasibility and Scalability:** Is the innovation technically and economically feasible? Can it be scaled for broader implementation?

Using the 4Ps framework as an assessment tool at innovation gates can ensure a comprehensive evaluation that considers the multifaceted nature of innovation and creativity. It helps in making informed decisions about whether to proceed, pivot, or pause a project, ensuring that resources are allocated effectively and increasing the chances of successful innovation. By systematically assessing each dimension, organizations can identify strengths, uncover potential issues, and make necessary adjustments to guide the innovation toward success. While this further details the process we already discussed in Chapter 4, the same issues with that model still apply, and we need to be careful as we implement these types of frameworks.

Wallace's creative process

One of the most comprehensive frameworks that influenced our understanding of the creative process was presented by Frank X. Wallace in the 1920s. Wallace's model describes the creative process as a series of four stages: Preparation, Incubation, Illumination, and Verification. It aimed to provide insight into how individuals come up with ideas that are both original and valuable in a structured way to aid in visualizing them without losing sight of the organic nature of the process. We will describe each one of those stages below (Figure 5.2).

Stage one: Preparation

The first stage is where the foundation for creative thinking all starts. In this stage, individuals actively gather information related to the problem, domain, or creative vision they are focusing on. By researching,

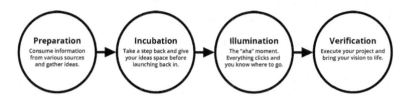

Figure 5.2 Wallace's creative process.

learning, or engaging deeply with the subject matter, we build a repository of information on the topic at hand. An artist, for example, could be studying techniques or exploring themes; a scientist could be analyzing existing theories and experiments. This stage equips us with the knowledge and tools that we will need to create something novel. Preparation doesn't only require taking in input, it also involves active engagement with the material in the form of questioning, critical analysis, and sorting of that information in ways that enable the stages to come. This is the starting point where we usually start making connections and recognizing patterns that are not immediately obvious.

Stage two: Incubation

On the surface level, this stage is less active. During incubation, we take a step back from the problem at hand and let our subconscious mind do all the work. This doesn't mean that we forget about what the problem is entirely; rather that we are not actively trying to come up with a solution. It's in the back of our minds as we go about with our lives. The incubation period is crucial because this allows for our DMN (see Chapter 1) and our subconscious to do *unconscious processing*. The mind starts making connections and associations that might not be possible through regular, active conscious thought. We approach incubation individually differently. For some of us, it can involve engaging in a different activity altogether. For others, it might be a short period of rest, a walk, or a shower. This might bring to mind our designers' answers in Chapter 2 about where they come up with ideas. Many of them were actually referring to the incubation period as the point in time where the idea first came to life. In incubation, the problem is simmering in the background, and the mind is allowed the time and space to wander without judgment and come back with results of its own in seemingly mystical ways.

Stage three: Illumination

This stage is often the most dramatic one, and it's what is typically associated with creativity. It's the "aha" moment when the solution or idea suddenly comes to the forefront. It's the most unpredictable stage as it can occur at any time and place. The idea emerges seemingly out of nowhere, though it's the result of the unconscious processing of information during the incubation phase. The solution or idea might not be fully formed just yet, but the key insight is evident. Illumination is often described as a moment of clarity and excitement, it's the reward of the hard work of preparation and the patience of incubation.

Stage four: Verification

The final stage is where the idea is tested and refined. This is where the idea is evaluated and is considered critically. This is where we contemplate our context and originality of the idea, work out the details, and consider how applicable and appropriate it truly is. This is where a scientist starts conducting experiments to test the theory and refine it based on those results, or when a game developer starts prototyping and tweaking the core concept based on how they playtested their results. Verification is crucial because it ensures that the idea is not only novel but also valuable and applicable. This is probably the most labor-intensive part of the creative process, as it requires meticulous attention to detail and willingness to revise and improve. The major creative problem is solved at illumination, and in verification is where all the ramifications of that solution are dealt with, refined, and improved.

Wallace's model highlights that creativity is a process that is about bringing an idea to fruition. It's a cycle of learning, thinking, stepping back, and then critically evaluating and improving an idea. It's a useful tool while practicing creative sobriety. The creative process is not just a stroke of genius that happens to a gifted few but can also become a process that can be nurtured and developed.

For instance, you can use that framework as a lens through which you can examine your own creativity. Which parts of your life are nurturing in which of the four stages? How can your work culture expand and cultivate the reach of one of the stages over the other? Are you having enough time to engage in different activities and allow your mind to wander? Moreover, when your mind does wander, are you allowing it to do so without judgment?

Wallace's model was a breakthrough in the understanding of the creative process early in the 20th century. However, it represents the creative process as a linear one, with one stage leading directly to the next. The creative process can be more organic and chaotic than that. Oftentimes, the stages can interlace or come across in different order. Moreover, it might not capture ideas that are generated without thorough understanding and preparation or creativity that is discovered in more organic ways or coming from a more personal viewpoint, which makes it useful to consider other frameworks alongside it.

The Geneplore's model

Cognitive psychologists Ronald A. Finke, Thomas B. Ward and Steven M. Smith presented the Geneplore model in the 1990s, which is often celebrated for its simplicity and profound depth. It encapsulates the essence of creativity through two main phases: the generative phase and the exploratory phase. It postulates that creativity is a cyclical process where individuals alternate between generating and exploring ideas, hence the name "Geneplore" (Figure 5.3).

Generative phase

Here the focus is on producing a wide range of raw and unfiltered ideas, concepts, or mental images also known as *preinventive structures.* These structures are not fully formed solutions but will act as seeds for creativity to grow. In this phase, you are encouraged to exercise divergent thinking, make as many novel connections and break away from traditional patterns of thought to explore a wide array of possibilities. In this phase, artists sketch without a clear end in mind, scientists hypothesize only theoretically, and musicians just play their instrument without predetermined purpose. This phase doesn't concern itself with outcome, but with generating a diverse pool of ideas that can then be evaluated, refined, developed further, or discarded altogether.

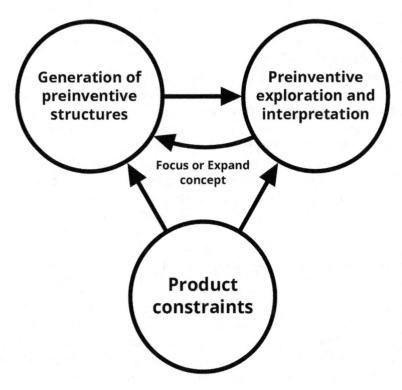

Figure 5.3 The Geneplore model.

Exploratory phase

Here the focus shifts from generating ideas to evaluating, refining, and elaborating on them. This is where we start to scrutinize the ideas we have in the pool, and switch from divergent thinking to convergent. The ideas are developed into a more complete, coherent, and practical. This phase utilizes a lot more problem solving and analytical thinking as we assess the viability, relevance and potential of an idea that was previously generated. Here the musician can take a simple melody and develop it into a song or a more complex musical composition; or an inventor might take a prototype and work out the practicalities to turn it into a product people can use. The exploratory phase involves not just filtering out the best ideas but also refining and combining ideas in novel ways. It's about understanding the implications, potential applications, and limitations of an idea over multiple cycles of revision of reevaluation until the idea is honed into its final form.

The Geneplore model highlights that the creative process is iterative. It's not a linear journey from one phase to another but a cyclical process of generation and exploration. After exploring our initial pool of ideas, we might return to the generative phase to come up with new ideas based on the new conclusions we have learned. It's continuously evaluating and evolving ideas, which in turn supports the unpredictable nature of the creative process itself.

The model further highlights the influence of knowledge, and our personal experience is on creativity. Ideas in the pool of ideas in the generative phase are influenced by our existing knowledge, experience, and life journey. That means that the knowledge we acquire in the exploration phase is added to our life journey then will no doubt *inspire* us to come up with even more ideas. Our reinterpretation of existing knowledge in new ways enriches our life experience. When we ponder and practice creative sobriety and understand ourselves further, it allows us to generate even more ideas, which is why we return to the generative phase with new perspectives and output. Our creative potential is enhanced by participating in the creative process itself. The more we come with ideas, the more we generate ideas about those ideas and how to use them.

"People always ask us whether we take risks on purpose. But to us, we don't really take risks – we just keep trying new things", said Nintendo's Shinya Takahashi in an interview with *The Guardian* (2018) where he was giving some insight into the creative process at Nintendo. "The thinking that guides us is: what can we do to pleasantly surprise players? It's not that we're consciously trying to innovate; we're trying to find ways to make people happy. The result is that we come up with things other people have not done."

The method Nintendo uses to find these new ideas relies on using small teams, giving them a direction and empowering them to engage with the generative and exploration phases to come up with as many ideas as possible.

In many cases, we begin by assigning a small group to a project; not necessarily senior staff, but developers, to try and come up with ideas. Those lead to the end product. *Super Mario*

Odyssey is a good example to explain this: we actually had several small groups, and as a result, we had many different ideas, which we then put together to make a single product. Naturally, during the course of early development, we find the right mission for each project. I believe every game has a different mission. With [Nintendo Switch launch game] 1–2 Switch, for example, the mission was to make a party game where players would not have to look at the screen—where people would face each other. (Guardian News and Media, 2018)

While Wallace's model provides a sequential overview of the stages of creativity, the Geneplore model offers a cyclical view, suggesting that individuals often iterate between generating and exploring ideas. This reflects the real-world creative process more accurately, where creators might go back and forth between thinking up new possibilities and critically evaluating them, sometimes revisiting earlier stages as new insights are gained.

Auteurship

In film theory, an auteur is a leading creative force that holds a distinctive, personal style and vision of the project. This is a term that is increasingly relevant in the gaming industry as individual creators—often designers or directors—leave strong and identifiable marks on their work. We've mentioned several of them at different parts of this book so far, from Hideo Kojima to Shigeru Miyamoto and Keita Takahashi. Their games exemplify the significant impact a single visionary can have on game development. Their creative forces are intensely personal and often non-conventional and therefore instantly recognisable.

Working with an auteur has its advantages, as their strong and clear vision can lead to the creation of truly unique and innovative gaming experiences that stand out in a very competitive and crowded market. They tend to push boundaries by challenging conventions and elevating the medium's artistic potential. They inspire their teams to achieve higher standards of creativity and excellence; their games are memorable and resonate with audiences on a very deep level due to their personal nature. Their name and reputation can also attract talent and create a buzz around their projects.

However, their singular vision and controlling nature can sometimes stifle the creativity and contributions of their team members, with work environments that are normally much more hierarchical. This can cause tensions and conflicts within the team, especially when the auteur's vision diverges significantly from the team's expertise and contributions. Auteur's tend to be uncompromising on their artistic vision, which causes conflicts and issues even outside of the team over budgets, timelines, and commercial viability. Their projects often overrun and are costly, with a risk of overindulgence in certain aspects at the expense of others, which might limit the game's appeal to a broader audience.

The success of the project becomes closely tied to the auteur's reputation and personal brand, meaning that any controversy or decline can significantly impact the project's success and team's morale.

There are many stories in game development about projects led by auteurs that were considered difficult by the team's who were developing them. The strive to perfection of the creative vision has its costs. On the other side, some of the most celebrated games of all time came from auteurs with intense and uncompromising personal visions. Their deeply personal games push the medium forward and can lead to innovations we haven't seen before. The role of the auteur and their creative processes will undoubtedly remain a topic of keen interest and debate, further reflecting the interplay between artistic vision and collaborative creation in team projects.

Team-based model

A stark contrast to the auteur approach is a model that is rooted in the belief that a diverse group of individuals, each with their unique perspectives and expertise can collectively create something that is more innovative and reflectively larger than the sum of its parts. Team-based model emphasizes teamwork, open communication, and shared vision, with each member contributing to all aspects of the game's development. It's a somewhat democratic process that enables every voice to be heard and feel valued.

Unlike the auteur approach, this model is based on the principle of collaboration and encourages active participation and input from all

members. Artists, programmers, writers, designers, and other specialists who work together from the inception of the game to its completion
all participate in making the creative decisions that make the game.
Group discussions, feedback loops, and brainstorming sessions (more
on that later this chapter) ensure that the game evolves in a way that
considers multiple viewpoints and is focused on the end experience of
the player while leveraging the collective creativity of the team.

Valve software is one of the largest video game developers and
publishers in the world based out of Seattle, famously promotes a flat
hierarchy where every developer in the team can contribute to their
project. They can simply wheel their desk and computer next to other
staff members and discuss how they want to contribute to the project
and can have an equal say on the project's creative direction. I once
asked one of Valve's level designers soon after the release of *Half-Life
2* about how they resolved conflicts if two members of the team had
opposite viewpoints. He answered that they simply playtest the two
approaches, and they would watch players try out the different
approaches and see which direction better suited the players and the
game. The player's experience was the ultimate judge for which creative direction to move toward.

With a diverse group of people contributing their ideas, games are
like to explore concepts and ideas that might not have emerged from a
single individual vision, which is perhaps the primary advantage of the
team-based model. The diversity of thought brought up from a range of
skills and expertise can lead to complex, nuanced, and engaging
games, as the team collectively solve problems and overcome challenges more effectively than a one person working alone.

Collaborative approach brings in more inclusive and representative
games. With team members from different backgrounds, cultures, and
experiences will inevitably reflect on the game experience, enhancing
the richness and depth of the end product and expanding its appeal.

The difficulty of applying this model, however, is the high potential
of conflict and disagreement among team members. With different perspectives and ideas, it's inevitable that not everyone will agree all the
time. Tensions, disputes, and slow decision-making can affect those
projects. Raising the need for effective communication, conflict resolu-
tion skills, and a clear decision-making process keep the project on
track.

Coordinating a large group of people and facilitating communication and reaching consensus on decisions can take time and slow down the development process, which is particularly challenging in a fast-paced industry where time to market is critical. Moreover, there's a higher risk of a diluted or inconsistent vision due to a lack of clear direction or cohesive style, which comes from disagreement of the team on the core vision, values, and goals of the project.

Despite these challenges, the collaborative team-based model offers a compelling alternative to the auteur one. By leveraging the collective creativity, skill sets, and perspectives of a diverse team, this model can lead to more innovation, engagement, and inclusive games that are more focused on the player experience than the self-expression of a sole creator. Though it'll require carful management and commitment to collaboration, there could be significant benefits to be reaped.

Contextual conception model

I have worked with creative leaders who have successfully managed to combine both approaches to get the best of both worlds as possible. Those leaders were practicing creative sobriety intuitively, they are fully aware that a hive mind of many will outweigh that of a single isolated mindset, and they believe in the power of harmony between team members as well as their ability to bring their own backgrounds, expertise, and knowhow will yield into more ideas in terms of quantity but also in terms of the originality of the ideas generated.

I'm calling that method Contextual Conception Model (CCM) which aims to create value, direction, originality, and cohesion, and the outline of it is as follows:

- **Define a Problem Space:** Give the team a clear problem to solve [defining the context in which the team operates or value]
- **Chart Vision Pillars:** Give the team a clear vision for their area [setting a clear direction for the team to follow]
  - o Give the responsibility to the team to come up with ideas in their field [foster the creative space for the team to arrive at innovation and originality]
- **Communicate the Vision:** Connect all ideas in one coherent big picture [create a sense of cohesion for the project]

I want to expand on each of those steps, as there's a lot of nuance to each and is worth exploring in detail.

Defining a problem space

When considering putting together the creative vision, it's important to consider the problem statement, which means to translate the vision pillars into desired design problems to be solved. An example of that could be determining the technical constraints of a project that could be by determining the target platform as before work started. An example of that could be your game is going to be designed for smartphones. That means that the design is to the smart phones input mechanisms, which include the touchscreen, gyroscope, microphone, or camera. Define the problem. State further means that the design problem is even a lot more focused. So for example, if that's a game for smartphones and it has to utilize the camera as an input device, then that means that whatever game will end up creating will be heavily utilized and become Therefore, the design team will know which part of the problem statement to focus on the design process.

To zoom out a little bit further, taking design pillars beyond mere technical as they could also be artistic constraints or desired expressions or emotions and whatever into, and then that also creates a type of creative constraint of a problem statement that the team will need to solve. An An example of that would be if the desired time feel of the game is to be uplifting and comedic, Then that by default rules out any design decision that could render the game to be frightening or dark or anything else that goes against that rule of thumb.

Albert Einstein said that if he had one hour to save the world, he would spend 55 minutes defining the problem. Charles F. Kettering, General Motors' Head of Research from 1920 to 1947, said "A problem well-defined is half-solved" (Freiesleben and Hartmann, 2023).

The principle of the method that I'm proposing is that at its core creative vision is creating constraints. Self-inflicted constraints or problems that need creative solutions for, and the more we spend time defining what are the problems statements that we are going to tackle along with our team, the more scalable the creative process becomes. Combining that with the creative sobriety exercise that we've gone through in earlier chapters means that the teams will have clear problems that they need to solve, and the method of reflection that allows them to create more original solutions to those problems.

So how do we create those vision and problem statements and how do we distribute them?

Vision pillars

Creative vision pillars refer to the fundamental principles or core ideas that guide and shape the development of a creative project. It's a set of statements that define for the project what it is and what it is not, serving as a foundation, providing a clear direction and purpose, and ensuring consistency and coherence throughout the process. They help teams stay aligned and focused, ensuring every decision contributes to the overarching vision of the project.

Authoring vision pillars is understanding the project's goals, audience, and core values; it is the output of discussions among the creative leadership team (often referred to as core team). It's about identifying what is most important for the project's success and what will set it apart. The chosen pillars should reflect the unique identity and aspirations of the project while being broad enough to guide various aspects of the creative process.

Vision pillars aren't designs; they are design challenges, so by definition, they are not solutions. Pillars don't define what is to be done, but the general law governs the decision process for anyone working on the project to run a check to see if their design or solution actually serves the greater picture of what the project is or not. Therefore, the choice of words and supporting material really matters because of how different people can't interpret things drastically differently than others. Defining the vision often includes defining an anti-vision, what the project is not.

Vision pillars are a framework for decision-making. They are the constraints that can be derived by factors that are either technical, audience-related, emotional, intellectual, or creative constraints-related.

Technical constraints

Technical constraints are the limitations imposed by various factors such as hardware capabilities, software tools, time, budget, and team expertise. These constraints are critical considerations in determining how well the creative team can realize their vision. If one of the vision pillars is to create a game with highly immersive environments, technical constraints like graphic processing capabilities and engine limitations might restrict the level of detail and interactivity possible. As such, while vision pillars represent the aspirational goals of the project, technical constraints define the practical boundaries within which these goals must be achieved. Balancing these will inevitably lead to innovative problem-solving, ensuring the vision is realized as closely as possible within the given limits.

Sometimes, the vision pillars can come from the team's desire to practically explore or showcase a particular technical breakthrough and make that one of the core focuses of the game. The aforementioned no loading screens pillar of God of War is one such example. Another is the approach followed in the development of *Doom 3*, the team at id Software wanted to utilize technology to create a horror-themed atmosphere, making lighting and shadows a key part of their vision. Despite hardware limitations of that time, they innovated with real-time dynamic lighting and stencil shadowing that created a frightening environment. In fact, speaking of horror, the fog we discussed before in *Silent Hill* games is another example that showcased how teams turn potential technical constraints into breakthroughs that became central to the game's vision and experience.

Intellectual property constraints

Intellectual Property (IP) constraints can shape the creative direction and become a vision pillar in game development. When working within the boundaries of an established IP, developers must respect the existing. lore, character designs, and world-building elements. This constraint can transform into a pillar by focusing on honoring and expanding the IP in innovative ways. Developers might emphasize fidelity to the original material while finding creative avenues to introduce fresh gameplay mechanics, storylines, or visual enhancements that respect and enrich the legacy. This approach ensures the game resonates with fans and retains the essence of the IP.

IP constraints also refer to the legal and branding guidelines that dictate how certain licensed or proprietary content can be used. These could stem from a game being part of a larger franchise, a collaboration with another entity, or any scenario where pre-existing creative content comes with a set of rules and expectations. Rather than viewing these constraints as mere hurdles, a forward-thinking team might position them as a foundational pillar of their creative vision, guiding the project's direction in a way that respects the original IP while also pushing creative boundaries. Recognizing and embracing these boundaries from the outset can lead to the deliberate crafting of a game experience that is both familiar and fresh, blending respect for the original material with new, exciting elements.

The gaming industry is filled with examples of games that have managed that successfully with clear IP constraints as part of their vision pillars, from Rocksteady's groundbreaking *Batman Arkham* series to Insomniac's *Spider-man* games, both games greatly embraced their protagonist and made the cerebral connection between the player and their masked vigilante a core game pillar. You can almost imagine that the player feeling like Batman or Spider-Man was a core vision pillar that the team took into account in all aspects of game creation as they were making those games.

Target audience-related constraints

Target audience constraints aim to guide developers to create relevant experiences for specific player groups. Understanding the unique preferences, abilities, and cultural contexts of the intended audience drives the development of games that resonate on a personal level with players. This requires understanding the interests and expectations of the target demographic, whether they are casual gamers seeking relaxation, hardcore players craving a challenge, or any other distinct group then making sure that the game being developed is suitable—valuable, perhaps—to the people that will play it.

Incorporating target audience constraints as a vision pillar ensures that games are culturally and emotionally impactful. It encourages developers to craft stories and characters that reflect the diversity and nuances of their audience, fostering a deeper connection and sense of representation. This focus on the audience also ensures games are accessible and considerate of various needs and sensitivities.

Having that constraint in mind while developing casual games on smartphones, for example, is why those games tend to have short and repeatable sessions, as the developers are aware that for those types of games, the player is on the go, they might be waiting for the bus, or in the doctor's office, so they want to be entertained as they're waiting, they can have a round or two until their turn is called or until they reach their stop. That vision pillar challenges the designers with such design problems as "how can we make an entertainment experience that it's captivating start to finish in under 2 minutes?" or "how can we create an experience so intuitive that someone can understand it at a glance and start playing if they only had 2 or 3 minutes to play?" Answering those questions requires great finesse in design, creative problem solving, and testing. Understanding the importance of that creative pillar is the responsibility of the core team and will effectively guide the progress of the project from then on.

Emotional constraints

Emotional constraints as a vision pillar put the focus back on the end user or player, specifically how we as game developers want them to *feel*. They are pillars that fundamentally aim to shape the player's journey, ensuring that experience is designed to evoke specific feelings and reactions. Think of them as clear emotional goals—be it fear in a survival horror, tranquility in a zen puzzle, or camaraderie in a cooperative multiplayer—that allow developers to craft experiences that resonate deeply and create memorable moments because of how they trigger an emotional response. This focus on the intended emotional impact guides all aspects of game development, from storyline and character development to gameplay mechanics and sound design. It ensures that every element works in harmony to deliver the desired emotional experience, making the game more immersive and engaging.

Integrating emotional constraints as a vision pillar also encourages innovation and empathy in design. Developers are challenged to explore novel ways of storytelling and interaction that can elicit complex emotions, which pushes the industry forward, encouraging games that not only entertain but also connect with players on an emotional level through experiences that stay with them long after they've put down the controller. Prioritizing the emotional journey allows games to transcend pure entertainment, becoming powerful mediums for storytelling, art, and personal expression.

Incorporating emotional constraints into the tone and feel of a game is essential for setting a cohesive and compelling creative vision. The tone of a game refers to its general character or attitude—whether it's dark and foreboding, light and whimsical, or somewhere in between. The feel, on the other hand, pertains to the tactile and sensory experience of playing the game. Together, they create an immersive atmosphere that can deeply influence a player's emotional journey.

When emotional constraints are tied to tone and feel, every aspect of the game—from the visual style and music to the narrative and gameplay mechanics—is carefully designed to evoke specific emotions. For example, a game intended to make players feel tension and fear might employ a dark, oppressive visual tone alongside suspenseful music and unpredictable gameplay. Conversely, a game designed to elicit joy and relaxation might use bright, colorful graphics, soothing sounds, and gentle, flowing gameplay. The thoughtful integration of emotional constraints with tone and feel is a powerful tool for crafting meaningful and impactful gaming experiences.

Creative constraints

These constraints are reflections of the creators' unique styles, experiences, and philosophies, and when embraced, they drive originality and authenticity in game design. When articulated clearly, it becomes a distinctive fingerprint, differentiating the game by imparting a unique voice and perspective. We've covered these types of constraints earlier on when we discussed creative vision in various parts of this book. It is often whether or not auteurs are aware of it, the key constraints that they apply to their creations that set their projects apart from everything else.

By setting boundaries based on their preferences, creators can focus their efforts and resources on deepening and polishing the aspects of the game that resonate most with their vision. Usually the most challenging part of this for creators is to identify in words what those preferences are. Another reason I advocate the practice of creative sobriety. Becoming aware of one's own sources of inspiration, own preferences, and own views of the world to the point of being able to accurately articulate it means that one can form a set of constraints for others to function in. This is a key part of the contextual conception method that I am proposing here. It's an output of deep introspection that comes from creative sobriety, understanding as a creator what my preferences are but more importantly why do I prefer them. What were the events and experiences of my life journey that have led me to arrive at said preferences are the combination of elements that lead to which enabling for more original thought, and therefore, how can I clearly articulate it in a way that people can understand, and therefore, apply to their everyday work?

Games developed under the guidance of strong creative constraints often have a coherent and cohesive feel, with every element from the storyline to the visual aesthetics working in harmony to support the overarching vision. This coherence enhances the player's emotional engagement, making the game a more memorable and impactful experience. In essence, creative constraints, when leveraged as a vision pillar, drive the creation of video games that are not only coherent and focused but also innovative and emotionally resonant. In the best of cases, it'll also transcend the end product to becoming culturally significant, as it's something that can be identified with given its strong creative focus.

Communicating a vision

Communicating the vision is vital as it serves as the guiding star for an entire team or project, ensuring everyone is moving in the same direction with a shared purpose. When the vision is clearly articulated and understood, it helps team members understand what they are doing and more importantly why they are doing it, giving them a sense of agency, empowerment, and fostering a deeper sense of purpose and motivation. This clarity reduces confusion and misalignment. Even more, a well-communicated vision inspires and motivates. It helps people see beyond their day-to-day tasks to the bigger picture and their role in achieving something larger than themselves. It sparks creativity and drives initiative as team members feel more connected to the end goal and are more likely to innovate and propose solutions aligned with the vision.

Clear communication of the vision is crucial for consistency in decision-making and messaging, both internally and externally. It ensures that all actions and communications are cohesive and support the desired end state. In times of change or uncertainty, a well-communicated vision is an anchor that stabilizes the team and a beacon of direction that guides them through challenges and keeps everyone focused on the ultimate goals.

Communicating creative vision pillars effectively is crucial for ensuring that everyone involved in a project understands and shares the same goals and expectations. Here's how to do it effectively:

1. **Clear Vision Pillar:** Begin by precisely defining each vision pillar. These are the foundational statements that will guide the project informed by the many different types of constraints we detailed earlier in this chapter. You must articulate these ideas in a way that is not only clear but also compelling and inspiring. Use descriptive language, anecdotes, or metaphors that resonate with the team. It's crucial to ensure that these pillars while abstract concepts are tangible enough for everyone to understand and relate to. For example, instead of saying a game should feel "exciting," describe the type of excitement—is it the thrill of discovery, the tension of a close race, or the adrenaline of a battle? The use of metaphors and analogies can help a lot in getting concepts across.

2. **Visual Representation:** We are visual creatures, a picture is worth a thousand words. Create detailed concept art, comprehensive mood boards, and other visual representations that capture the essence of each vision pillar. These visuals should reflect the game's intended style, mood, and atmosphere, providing a clear, visual benchmark for the direction. This might include color palettes that evoke certain emotions, character sketches that reflect the game's personality, or scene renderings that showcase the world's ambiance. Regularly update and refer to these visuals to keep the team aligned with the vision.

3. **Narrative and Storytelling:** Stories have the power to engage and inspire. Develop a rich narrative around the vision pillars that encapsulates the game's world, characters, key events, and emotional arcs. This should be more than just a plot summary; it should be a vivid, engaging story that brings the vision pillars to life. Share this narrative in an immersive way—perhaps through a written

document, a spoken presentation, or even a storyboard. The goal is to make the team feel connected to the game's story and motivated to bring it to life.

4. **Regular Meetings and Discussions:** Communication should be ongoing and dynamic. Hold regular meetings dedicated to discussing the vision pillars, their implementation, and any challenges faced. These shouldn't be one-sided lectures but are interactive sessions where questions are encouraged and are discussions where creative leaders are exercising active listening. Use these meetings to revisit the vision pillars, assess how well they are being integrated into the project, and make adjustments as needed. It's also a chance to celebrate successes and innovative ways team members have embodied the vision in their work.

5. **Documentation:** Comprehensive and accessible documentation is often neglected in practice, but it is what sets successful teams apart from others. Create detailed documents that outline the vision pillars, the rationale behind them, and how they should influence various aspects of the project. This might include specific guidelines, examples of how the pillars have been or can be implemented, and any other resources that might help the team understand and embrace the vision. This documentation should be a living document, regularly updated as the project evolves and new insights are gained. Make sure it's easily accessible to all team members, perhaps through a shared digital space.

6. **Lead by Example:** Leadership is about action, not just words. The leaders and key members of the team should exemplify the vision pillars in everything they do. This means making decisions, giving feedback, and creating work that reflects the core vision. When team members see leaders consistently embodying the vision pillars, they are more likely to understand and adopt these principles themselves. This also means being open about the process, sharing how you as a leader are making decisions based on the vision pillars, and the impact these decisions have. I believe that as a leader, your job is to serve your team. Consistently think about how you could better do that, how is your time utilized to better serve your team members, and how could you better enable them to best perform.

7. **Feedback Loop:** Establish a robust feedback loop. Encourage team members to regularly share how they are interpreting and implementing the vision pillars in their work. This might be through formal mechanisms like regular check-ins and reviews, or more informal methods like a suggestion box or open office hours. The goal is to create a two-way conversation where team members feel heard and leaders gain insights into how the vision is being received and integrated. This feedback loop is also an opportunity to identify misunderstandings, discover innovative applications of the vision pillars, and make adjustments as needed.

8. **Prototypes and Demos:** Sometimes, seeing is believing. Develop prototypes, demos, or other tangible representations that embody the vision pillars. These should be key pieces that showcase what the final product will look, feel, and play like. They serve as a concrete example that the team can reference and aspire to. Review these prototypes regularly, discussing how they align with the vision pillars and where improvements can be made. These can especially come in handy when the project under development is complex, with some aspects of it difficult to benchmark or never been seen before. Prioritize making these particular aspects visible to the team as soon as possible, those tend to be the parts that confuse the most and drag production along.

9. **Consistency and Reinforcement:** We often say half of a creative directors' job is to say the same things over and over again. Reiteration is key to internalization. Regularly reinforce the vision pillars through all communication channels—meetings, emails, casual conversations, and team updates. However, this doesn't mean just repeating the same words; it means consistently demonstrating and referring to the pillars in various contexts, showing how they are relevant to every aspect of the project. This continuous reinforcement helps to keep the vision at the forefront of everyone's mind and ensures that it remains a guiding force throughout the project. Take note whenever an aspect of a project is embodying the vision pillars, and amplify that.

10. **Flexibility and Openness:** While it's important to have a clear vision, it's also crucial to be adaptable. Creative projects will evolve in unexpected ways, and new insights or challenges will emerge.

Be open to adapting the vision pillars as the project progresses. This doesn't mean losing sight of the core vision but rather refining and evolving it in response to new information and circumstances. Encourage the team to be open to change and to view the vision as a living concept that grows and improves over time.

By expanding on these points, the process of communicating creative vision pillars becomes more detailed and nuanced, providing a comprehensive framework for guiding a team through the complex journey of bringing a creative vision to life.

It's critical that throughout the lifecycle of the project, and through regular discussions, meetings, feedback loops and other methods mentioned earlier that creative leaders are constantly updating the vision. This is another output of practicing creative sobriety. If a piece of feedback is common and recurring from players and team members alike, it's worthwhile exploring the underlying reasons behind it and consider if the vision should be updated to reflect it. If better ways are presented to articulate certain pillars, making an update and informing the team of why that update was made is an important factor. The vulnerability and flexibility shown is often welcomed by the team, as they feel their contributions going all the way to the top and affecting the vision of the project as a whole. How often should creative leaders stick to their vision in the face of feedback is a creative dilemma and is a topic that we will discuss at length in the next and final chapter of this book.

Updating a creative vision is a change management process every time, that requires the involvement of the team and stakeholders, they need to be part of that journey and buy into it. It's important to provide support during that change and paint a compelling picture of the future.

Creative leadership, setting the vision, and communication is an integral part of the creative process. It's one that needs to be handled with care and is iterative in its nature that requires it to be constantly revisited time and time again.

Generating ideas

An observation I had while teaching and especially in that idea generation exercise I mentioned earlier where students are supposed to come up with game ideas coming from either their everyday life or childhood as some students were mentioning their idea, others would comment saying "oh that's really cool, you can also make the player do this in your game too like that character from that movie." Just hearing someone else's idea caused others to get inspired and tried to figure out ways to create using it plus whatever other ingredient that they made a connection with (in that case a movie). Every time someone pitched an idea, others would say how much it reminded them of something else but with a twist, even if they didn't get the intention entirely, the connection was established and they're already creating a different thing entirely in their mind. This applies to professional game devs as well. I have never pitched a game idea or seen someone pitching a game idea to someone else, without the other person immediately saying how much it reminded them of another game or something else they've experienced that is similar or not even connected. Or they would even start building to the idea with others of their own instantly, saying things like how it would be cool if it was combined with something else.

Generating ideas in itself is inspirational and encourages further idea creation.

This is precisely why brainstorming is so effective, as you would place yourself in an environment that allows for unlimited idea creation. Once present in that environment, ideas connect to others, and they're all listed for someone to use as inspiration ingredients that can either present a design solution, a new perspective, or even a list of all items that people can think of around a certain topic.

Brainstorming

Brainstorming is a collaborative problem-solving method aimed at generating a wide array of ideas and solutions for a specific issue or topic. This creative technique emphasizes the free flow of thoughts, encouraging participants to think openly and propose as many ideas as possible, regardless of how unconventional they may be. The central premise is to explore an extensive range of perspectives and solutions without the immediate constraints of criticism or judgment, allowing creativity to flourish spontaneously.

The concept of brainstorming was first formalized by Alex Osborn in the 1940s. He introduced the term "brainstorming" in his 1942 book

How to Think Up (1942) and further elaborated on the technique in his 1953 book, *Applied Imagination.* The term "brainstorm" itself was meant to signify the fierce activation of creativity during these sessions where a "storm" of ideas are raging in the brain.

Often conducted in group settings, brainstorming sessions are designed to create an open and inclusive atmosphere where every participant feels encouraged to contribute their thoughts. Typically, a facilitator guides the discussion, ensuring that the conversation remains focused and that everyone gets a chance to participate. One of the key aspects of brainstorming is prioritizing the quantity of ideas over their quality. The belief is that generating a high volume of ideas increases the likelihood of discovering a robust and innovative solution. The longer these sessions get, the further away the group will step away from level 1 or inevitable ideas that we discussed in Chapter 3 and delve into deeper levels of associative thoughts.

During these sessions, criticism and evaluation of ideas are intentionally postponed. This approach encourages free thinking and minimizes the fear of judgment, which can inhibit creativity and lead to more conventional ideas. Participants are urged to welcome unusual and out-of-the-box ideas. Brainstorming is not just about proposing individual ideas; it's also about building on others' suggestions. Participants are encouraged to combine and improve on ideas presented by their peers. This collaborative approach can lead to more refined and comprehensive solutions, as different viewpoints and knowledge bases come together to enhance the original proposals.

Brainstorming is a versatile technique used across various contexts, from business and education to personal projects. It is particularly beneficial in the early stages of a project or when a problem requires fresh and inventive thinking. Effective brainstorming not only yields a diverse array of potential solutions but also fosters team building and enhances creative thinking skills among participants. It's a dynamic process that, when facilitated well, can unlock the collective creativity and problem-solving capabilities of any group. This is where diverse team dynamics can come into play, when there are many different perspectives present, the output will be widespread and capture a large spectrum of creative output.

The main criticisms of brainstorming are often on how the participants take part in the exercise, one example is the phenomenon of "social loafing", where individuals in a group might put in less effort, assuming others will contribute. Another issue is "production blocking", where only one person can speak at a time in a group setting, potentially limiting the free flow of ideas, sometimes that could lead to anchoring, where one voice is taking more space, causing conformity amongst other participants and limiting the creative output of the group. Most of these criticisms come from social dynamics within the participants, therefore, it's critical for facilitators - often the creative leaders themselves—to be able to understand the social dynamic of the group and pick the brainstorming method that suits that dynamic the most.

These methods aim to mitigate these criticisms and enhance the effectiveness of the sessions. There are numerous brainstorming techniques, each designed to encourage creativity and idea generation in different ways. Here's a list briefly describing each of those techniques:

- **Traditional Brainstorming:** This classic approach presented by Osborn involves a group coming together to freely generate a multitude of ideas around a specific topic. The key is to prioritize quantity over quality and to create an environment where judgment is suspended, and all contributions are welcomed. Participants are also encouraged to build on each other's ideas leading to unexpected and innovative solutions. To facilitate this process effectively, it's crucial to have a skilled moderator who can keep the session focused and ensure that all voices are heard. Traditional brainstorming is particularly beneficial when you want to generate a large number of ideas quickly and have a diverse group with different perspectives.

- **Brainwriting:** This method addresses some of the common challenges of group brainstorming, such as production blocking and evaluation apprehension, by having participants write down their ideas independently before sharing them with the group. This can be done using paper, index cards, or digital tools. After a set period, the ideas are collected and then discussed or built upon by others. Brainwriting ensures that quieter group members have an equal chance to contribute and can lead to a more diverse set of ideas. It also allows participants time to think more deeply about their contributions and avoids anchoring as participants are not influenced by others' inputs yet as they write down their ideas (Figure 5.4).

- **Round-Robin Brainstorming:** To ensure equitable participation, this technique has each member of the group share an idea in turn. This process continues until the flow of ideas starts to repeat or slow down. Round-Robin Brainstorming is particularly effective in groups where dominant personalities might otherwise overshadow quieter members. It ensures that everyone has a chance to contribute, which can lead to a more comprehensive exploration of the problem at hand. Additionally, hearing a wide range of ideas voiced one after the other can spark new thoughts and connections that might not arise in a more free-form discussion. This is the technique

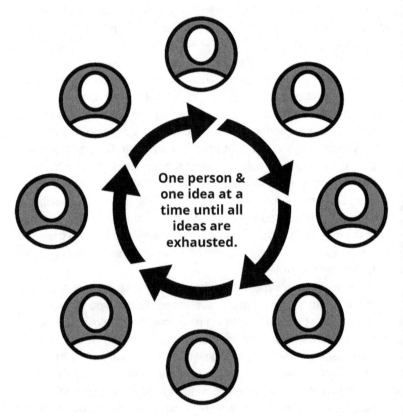

Figure 5.4 Round-Robin brainstorming.

I often use in illustrating my creative sobriety concept presented in Chapter 3, when I start with the notion of color and ask participants in turn to contribute one idea at a time under a very rapid time limit.

- **Mind Mapping:** Mind mapping begins with a central idea or problem and expands outward with branches representing related concepts, words, and ideas. This visual technique helps participants see the relationships between different ideas and can lead to a deeper understanding of the problem and more creative solutions. It's particularly useful when dealing with complex issues that have multiple components or when you want to explore the breadth and depth of a topic. As the map grows, patterns and new connections often emerge, leading to insights that might not be apparent in a more linear discussion. We have already presented the concept of mind mapping in detail in Chapter 3 of this book, this is a brainstorming technique that applies it to a group exercise setting (Figure 5.5).

- **Starburst Brainstorming:** Starbursting focuses on generating questions about the problem or idea at the center of the brainstorming session. Participants create questions starting with who, what, where, when, why, and how, exploring the issue from

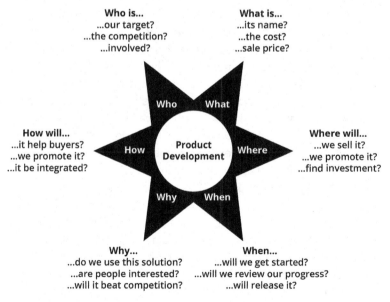

Figure 5.5 Starbursting brainstorming.

multiple angles. This technique helps uncover various aspects of the problem and can lead to a more comprehensive and nuanced understanding. It's particularly useful in the early stages of problem-solving when you're still defining the scope and scale of the issue. By focusing on questions rather than solutions, Starbursting can also help prevent premature convergence on a single idea and encourage a more thorough exploration. This method is especially helpful in narrowing down on creative vision pillars as they are more abstract notions, by focusing on defining the problem statement rather than solutions.

- **Reverse Brainstorming:** This technique turns the problem on its head by asking participants to think of ways to cause or exacerbate the issue. By deliberately thinking about the worst-case scenarios or negative outcomes, participants can uncover underlying assumptions about the problem. Once a range of negative ideas has been generated, the group can then discuss how to prevent or address these scenarios, often leading to innovative and outside-the-box solutions. Reverse Brainstorming is particularly effective when dealing with persistent problems that have resisted more straightforward solutions.

- **Role Storming:** In Role Storming, participants adopt different personas and generate ideas from these perspectives. For example, they might take on the role of a customer, a competitor, a regulator, a player, or someone from a completely unrelated field. This technique encourages empathy and can lead to a deeper understanding of the needs and motivations of different stakeholders. Participants can come up with more varied and innovative ideas because they are stepping out of their comfort zone. Role Storming is particularly useful when trying to understand a problem from all sides or when looking for creative ways to meet diverse needs (Figure 5.6).

- **The Stepladder Technique:** This method starts with a small core group discussing the problem. Additional members are then introduced one by one, with each new member having some time to think about the issue independently before joining the discussion. This ensures that each person can contribute fresh ideas without being influenced by the group's direction. The Stepladder Technique can help prevent groupthink and ensure that all perspectives are considered. It's particularly useful when you have a larger group

Five Steps of The Stepladder Technique

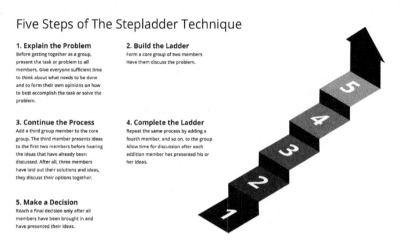

1. Explain the Problem
Before getting together as a group, present the task or problem to all members. Give everyone sufficient time to think about what needs to be done and to form their own opinions on how to best accomplish the task or solve the problem.

2. Build the Ladder
Form a core group of two members. Have them discuss the problem.

3. Continue the Process
Add a third group member to the core group. The third member presents ideas to the first two members before hearing the ideas that have already been discussed. After all, three members have laid out their solutions and ideas, they discuss their options together.

4. Complete the Ladder
Repeat the same process by adding a fourth member, and so on, to the group. Allow time for discussion after each addition member has presented his or her ideas.

5. Make a Decision
Reach a final decision only after all members have been brought in and have presented their ideas.

Figure 5.6 The stepladder technique.

or when you want to ensure that more introverted members have a chance to contribute.

- **Figure Storming:** Figure Storming involves imagining how someone else would solve a problem. Participants pick a well-known figure, such as a historical leader, fictional character, or even a colleague, and brainstorm ideas from their perspective. This approach encourages creative thinking by pushing participants to step outside their usual problem-solving approaches and consider different values, knowledge, and skills. It can be particularly useful for generating unconventional solutions and for teams that feel stuck in their usual ways of thinking. Sometimes, the figures themselves are brainstormed before the session and distributed randomly to the participants, adding entertainment to the session but also making sure everyone is on their toes and has their creativity further stimulated.
- **Rapid Ideation Brainstorming:** Rapid Ideation is a time-constrained exercise where participants are challenged to generate as many ideas as possible within a short period. This technique forces a focus on quantity over quality and can help break through creative blocks by encouraging spontaneous thinking. After the rapid ideation session, the ideas are reviewed, and the most promising ones are developed further. This technique is particularly useful when you

need a large volume of ideas quickly or when you want to energize a group and encourage bold thinking.

Each of these techniques offers a different approach to brainstorming, and the best choice will depend on the specific context, including the nature of the problem, the composition of the group, and the desired outcomes. Mixing and matching different methods is also encouraged, as it helps keep the situation novel and avoids stagnation. More importantly, it allows facilitators more tools on their belt to navigate a wide variety of social contexts of these sessions.

Many people ask me how I come up with ideas for my projects, while the genesis of them is mostly either from reflecting on personal experiences or by a problem statement (usually in the form of my manager assigning me to deliver on a project) the refinement of the ideas and how I want to tackle specific problems and designs comes from me talking to people. I usually approach the people I respect for their opinions as I'm first forming the idea and take their input in, I then continue to do so for the entirety of the project, I'm often talking to people about the project that I'm working regardless of how well developed it is, it's because exactly like in brainstorming when I present people my ideas they'll either have an emotional reaction or it'll trigger their inspiration pools and they'll start to tell me about what my idea reminds them of.

Emotional reactions are generally a very good indication if I'm on the right track or not, the emotional reaction could be universally negative which means that I must practice creative sobriety and reconsider. Either my approach in presenting the idea or even the idea itself, I need to have humbleness and open-mindedness to accept both equally, as well as a possibility of a third reason that I haven't considered yet. Co-Author of *Rules of Play* Eric Zimmerman once told me "critique is the highest form of flattery", I consider every feedback I get as such. If the emotional reaction is positive, either praise, agreement, or in the best case inspiration! That's usually in the form of people listening to me getting activated by the idea I'm presenting and they start to view their own work through that lens. When this situation happens, and my ideas start inspiring people for a different way to view their own work, it generally means that I am on to something.

I first had the idea for this book when I was watching a talk my dear ex-colleague Stephen Jarret did on analogous inspiration and how that influenced his approach to leading and inspiring our game design teams in the company in which we both worked at the time. Ironically, his talk inspired me to dig deeper into the topic of analogous inspiration, and with that in mind, I started to get observations and thought experiments on how designers and students came up with ideas, many examples of which you've come across in this book, I wanted to back those observations with studies I've done on psychology and neuroscience. As soon as I thought I had something, I started putting the main ideas that I had in the form of a presentation on the creative process, presenting in various game development conferences around the world. The positive reaction I got from the audience confirmed that my findings on the topic I'm presenting are something that resonates with a lot of people in my field, the enthusiasm of the audience, or the debates that started following my talks or the number of inquiries I received afterward from people wanting to know more. On the other hand, I also started getting similar questions in the Q&A sessions following my talks, which led me to think that no doubt the reader will have similar questions. So I started studying, researching, and coming up with conclusions and answers to those questions which ended up being the bulk of the material of this book. In many ways, I was playtesting this book before it was printed, and no doubt the final result will also spark debates, criticism, and discussion that will push me toward finding answers to those as well. The countless discussions and debates I had about the material here in addition to my experience making games and teaching game development were all sparks of inspiration that I could pull throughout the creative process here as well.

This book is a result of my personal life journey and experiences, starting from the initial spark of curiosity on the topic of analogous inspiration, to observations I conducted at class or at work, to brainstorming with many industry colleagues around the world, to the iteration and incremental improvement. I wanted to use the process I followed to make this book and bring it to the reader as a demonstration of the creative process and how inspiration works. The very content of this book explains how it came to be, just like any other example in it.

Further Reading

Ferch, S.R., & Song, J. (2023). Create dangerously. *The International Journal of Servant-Leadership*, 17(1), 21–26.

Finke, R.A. (1996). Imagery, creativity, and emergent structure. *Consciousness and Cognition*, 5(3), 381–393.

Freiesleben, T. and Hartmann, S. (2023) What does explainable AI explain? Timo Freiesleben; Betreuer: Stephan Hartmann. München: Universitätsbibliothek der Ludwig-Maximilians-Universität.

Guardian News and Media. (2018). Inside Nintendo's secretive creative process. *The Guardian*. https://www.theguardian.com/games/2018/apr/25/nintendo-interview-secret-innovation-lab-ideas-working

Jung, C. (1921). *The Collected Works of C.G. Jung, volume 6: Psychological Types.*

Jung, C.G. (1968). *Collected works of C. G. Jung, volume 12: Psychology and alchemy.* Princeton University Press.

Jung, C.G., & Hull, R.F.C. (1960). *Synchronicity: An acausal connecting principle* (from vol. 8 of the collected works of C. G. Jung). Princeton University Press. https://www.jstor.org/stable/j.ctt7s94k

Linsey, J.S., & Becker, B. (2011). Effectiveness of brainwriting techniques: Comparing nominal groups to real teams. In *Design creativity 2010* (pp. 165–171). Springer London.

Osborn, A. F. (1942). *How to think up.* McGraw-Hill.

Osborn, A. F. (1953). *Applied imagination: principles and procedures of creative problem solving.* Charles Scribner's Sons.

Rhodes, M. (1961). An analysis of creativity. *The Phi delta Kappan*, 42(7), 305–310.

Rogelberg, S. G., Barnes-Farrell, J. L., & Lowe, C. A. (1992). The stepladder technique: An alternative group structure facilitating effective group decision making. *Journal of Applied Psychology*, 77(5), 730.

Thornblad, D. (2018). Managing innovation without managers: Valve Corp. *Journal of Case Studies*, 36(2).

Wallas, G. (1926). *The art of thought.* Harcourt, Brace.

Zane, L., & Zimbroff, A. & Matthews, C & Liguori, E (2021). Ideation techniques and applications to entrepreneurship. In *Annals of Entrepreneurship Education and Pedagogy–2021* (pp. 63–79). Edward Elgar Publishing.

Chapter 6

The creative dilemma

The object isn't to make art, it's to be in that wonderful state that makes art inevitable

—Robert Henry

Creativity is existential for us. Human innovation and technology that have helped improve our lives drastically, increase our life expectancy, and helped us organize our daily endeavors come directly through thoughts, discoveries, and inventions that existed because of the creativity of the people who made them. Inspired even if in part or accidentally by the works of those who came before them. In many ways, it's the responsibility of each and every one of us to take the learning that humanity has had through the ages, get inspired by it and create. We owe it to humanity to create, our role is to push humanity further even with just a line of poetry, a curious observation, or a musing theory. Our collective incremental output through time is what allows us as a species to evolve.

Rabindranath once said, "The one who plants trees, knowing that they will never sit in their shade, has at least started to understand the meaning of life." There is a universality of creative output. What we put together and send out, the universe will exist with the rest of human creation. Within it could lie a spark that will ignite a raging flame in someone else's imagination—maybe centuries after we're all long gone.

To be creative is a responsibility that we don't even know that we bear, but we carry it nonetheless. Creative minds often don't

DOI: 10.1201/9781003261834-6

understand or are able to articulate why they create, but they do know that they must. They feel within them the need to shout out a message that echoes through time. With good reason, that message is yet another piece of human collective intelligence that accumulates to eventually—and repeatedly—radically change our lives and the lives of those who come after us.

There were many examples and stories in this book that concluded—even if implicitly—with "and the rest was history". The world wasn't the same after Einstein's or Darwin's theories or Monet's paintings, or Miyamoto's games. While it might sound strange at first to group video games with the old masters or great scientists, it's entertainment at the end of the day. It did affect countless lives, however. Even creativity that produces what entertains us has an ever lasting effect on the world.

The year 1983 witnessed the largest and longest crash the video game industry has ever known as it lasted for two years. Revenues of the games industry were around three billion US dollars as of 1983 dropped to slightly less than 100 million US dollars in 1985, a steep drop of 97%. Many counted video games to have been a fad that has run its course. Many video game development and publishing companies went bankrupt. That crash was largely due to the oversaturated market, mostly with low-quality products. There were over ten different video games consoles from different manufacturers releasing many games as fast as possible for quick returns without adequate quality assurance practices. Luckily, the creativity of Nintendo and Miyamoto played a critical role in the revival of the industry with the release of the Famicom or Nintendo Entertainment System (NES) in 1985 featuring many of Miyamoto's creations such as Donkey Kong, Super Mario Bros, and The Legend of Zelda. An act of creation that aimed to entertain had an ever lasting impact on the world; it was one of the major factors why myself and many of the readers of this book are in the games industry to begin with. This conversation wouldn't have happened if it wasn't for an act of creation that happened back in the 1980s to create "mere entertainment".

Creativity affects our lives and those around us and those who come after us, in ways we can never fully fathom. We put out something that is part of the fabric of our time, culture, and society.

Vulnerability of creation

As we covered earlier in this book, whatever we create is coming from a place within us. It is a result of our personal life journey and how the world has touched us. Our history of experiences, knowledge, and life journey is all leading toward the idea that we formulate and want to act upon. It is something that is deeply personal. Nietzsche once said, "One must still have chaos in oneself to be able to give birth to a dancing star."

Under that light, then it makes a lot of sense why we feel precious and overly protective of our ideas. Why do a lot of creators feel any criticism of that idea as a personal attack. There's an inherent vulnerability when we want to ideate and create. It opens us to criticism, misunderstanding, and, in some cases, ridicule. It is exposing one's innermost thoughts, fears, desires, and hopes to the world. It's as if we are unveiling a part of our soul in our work.

Not only this, being truly creative can be an act of rebellion as bringing something new into existence challenges and reshapes the boundaries of what was previously known or understood. It's breaking free from the shackles of tradition, confronting and defying societal norms, and facing the vast uncertainty of the unknown. Erich Fromm declared that "creativity requires the courage to let go of certainties." It requires us to be vulnerable and rebellious.

The courage to create

Therefore, we need to have what Rollo May (1994) called *The Courage to Create* in his book of the same title. To create is not just to have an idea, but it's about having the courage to stand up for that idea, nurture it, and be willing to face both internal and external challenges to see it come to life. To May, we need to find a unique kind of courage, the courage to confront our fears, to tackle the unknown and mold chaos into order. To challenge ourselves, we make sense of our place in this vast universe. Creativity is existential on many different levels. It's what fuels the passion and determination of the creator for them to have a firm belief or understanding of their role in life, those who are in tune with their creative voice often grapple with questions about life's purpose, the nature of existence, and the mysteries of love and death. Their creative works are in some way a dialogue or a response with these profound quandaries. Albert Camus once said: "To create is to live twice."

Our openness about that part of us that could make us so susceptible to judgment is also the source of our work's authenticity and power. The genuineness of the thought is what resonates with those who engage with it. Henri Matisse often said, "Creativity takes courage." We need to know that in the face of all that judgment, we need to come out as authentic as possible. "To live a creative life, we must lose our fear of being wrong", as Joseph Chilton Pearce put it.

The courage to create comes from commitment. Unwavering belief in the importance of the message or the dedication to the craft. The true test of courage is persistence, to persevere with the idea in the face of fear, vulnerability, and doubt. "Creativity comes from trust. Trust your instincts. And never hope more than you work", wrote Rita Mae Brown (2011).

The courage to create also requires compassion towards ourselves. It is not easy to challenge fear head on, it is a difficult journey that requires resolve in the face of uncertainty. We need to be kind to ourselves, to accept that we will make mistakes, that we might be misunderstood and that we will falter along the way. The courage is to forgive ourselves and proceed, for to create is a journey that is well worth it.

The creative dilemma

Courage is not the absence of fear; it's the ability to proceed in spite of it. Our courage to create is for us to be mindful and acknowledge our fears then continue on to create knowing that they may indeed come to pass. The act of creation that we are carrying out and its place in the universe powers us through and strengthens our commitment to creation. Everything we've ever wanted is on the other side of fear.

That belief and commitment to the outcome despite the possibility of failure is what I'm calling the creative dilemma. It's not a problem as problems have solutions. A dilemma is a careful balance that needs to be taken into account as we proceed with our act of creation. It's our intuition and logic slow dancing in a burning room to borrow from John Mayer's song.

It's us believing in what we make despite the fear of failure, yet we exercise creative sobriety throughout our process to be grounded and be able to reassess clearly. Our only assurance that we are on the right path, is our ability to reflect. It's our belief that what we are expressing is coming from the uniqueness of our life journey, that we are practicing creative sobriety to drive our ideas deeper intellectually towards originality. It is our belief that we have weighed carefully all of our sources of inspiration and are making sober decisions in our journey toward the unknown.

Creativity means us confronting our truths including the very dilemma we are facing when we start the act of creation itself. It is not an act of escapism. It isn't about creating a fantasy world to run away from reality. It's about engaging more deeply with reality, seeing it from new perspectives, questioning it, challenging it, reshaping it, and exercising creative sobriety. The creator who avoids reality, who hides behind their work misses out on the transformative power of genuine creative engagement. "I have learned a great deal from listening carefully" said Ernest Hemingway. "Most people never listen."

Responsibility of creatives

Leonardo da Vinci once said: "The painter holds the brush in their hands and the universe in their mind." As we push forth ideas, perspectives or narratives in the world, we need to be aware that there are consequences to our actions. Creativity is acting on thoughts. Creativity also influences thought. It inspires further thought, but it also has a direct effect as it's part of the fabric of human output, our acts of creation influences culture and even at times the course of history itself. We hold multiple moral, ethical, and even kindness responsibilities toward ourselves and the world around us.

All creators need to be aware that as we are creating we need to have mindfulness. Mindfulness to what we create and why, the implications said creation might have. Our creation shouldn't be just a self-serving endeavor but something that is contributing positively to a wider human narrative.

Mindfulness also means that we become aware that we carry different types of responsibilities, to ourselves we owe authenticity, to humanity we owe it to be courageous, to the world around us we owe it ethical morality, and to our industry, we owe it creative sobriety.

To ourselves - authenticity

As creators, we are drawing inspiration directly from our personal life journey. We are aware of the choices and inputs that we have had to have led us to this point in time. We exercise creative sobriety and come to understand how the events and experiences have touched us. How the world touches us is a combination of feelings and perspectives that we have. We owe it to ourselves—and the work that we are creating—that we show vulnerability, that we show those feelings in the most unmasked way possible, that we do not alter them or modify them because we are opting to appease others. Dr Gabor Maté wrote in *The Myth of Normal* (2022) about how the pain of being authentic and not being accepted greatly outweighs the risk of the pain of seeking acceptance but not being ourselves. Our authenticity is something that others can feel in our work and it's what allows them to relate to it even more. Authenticity allows for the creation of works that translate feelings that others speak and don't speak of. We have a responsibility of ourselves to speak truthfully to those feelings and for others to benefit from that authenticity.

To May, as creators we all deal with a concept called staring into the abyss, as we at some point in our journey will confront a void, that is an overwhelming sense of emptiness, doubt or existential crisis. This abyss isn't necessarily negative, it can even be a necessary phase for the creation to come to pass. It requires us to face our darkest fears and doubts and allows us to break free from any superficial constraints (such as constricting ourselves from the fear of being judged or acting like someone that we're not for the desire to be accepted). The abyss challenges, it questions, but it also purifies, refining the creator's vision and purpose. What an opportunity it would be for us to stare into the abyss, and to accept it, and to be authentic in how we represent that journey.

To humanity - courage

We started this chapter by showcasing why creativity is an existential matter to us as humans. The importance of creativity is to how we developed as a species, and how the creativity of others inspires us and leads us to create something that may very well at some point change the course of history. Our creations can either do that directly, or through inspiring others at some point down the line for their creations to do that.

In order for us to do that then we must create. We owe that to mankind, but in order for us to create we need to show authenticity and vulnerability. We need to be aware that our ideas can cause us to be judged or even punished, yet continue to create despite those possibilities. We owe to mankind for us to have the courage to face our darkest fears within ourselves, realistic fears from society around us and stand up to that anxiety of creation by demonstrating courage. We understand that what we make might not amount to much, but go ahead and do it anyway.

To the world - ethics

Every act of creation carries an ethical weight. This is more true today than ever before, as creations and ideas have widespread impact and change our society norms right before our eyes. Societies, ecosystems, and even the very fabric of reality can change as a result of our creativity. Creators need to be mindful and consider the intent behind their creation as well as the potential repercussions. Our responsibility as creators is to take the ethical dimensions of our work seriously, even if we live in a material world that doesn't value it.

There are many ethical dimensions to consider, the scope of which would deserve a book of its own. I would like, however, to touch on some that are very important for our times. We should carefully consider the messages and themes our work promotes. Our creativity can shape public perception and behavior; thus, it's crucial to think about the values being communicated. Misrepresentation or the perpetuation of hateful messages can have deep societal impact beyond our immediate grasp. For example, depicting cultures or identities inaccurately perpetuates biases, creating prejudices against certain groups, alienates others, and in trying times divides us.

On the other end of that, ensuring that our work is accessible to those less fortunate than us, including those with disabilities, is part of our ethical responsibilities that unite us. Regardless if it's adding subtitles, providing translations, or designing games with adaptable controls. By making our creations accessible, we are creating with kindness in our hearts, and upholding the principle of equity, and our connection with humanity.

Carrying humanity in our heart is part of our ethical responsibility, when we're working towards creating something that has the potential to disrupt—as is currently with the huge investment in various artificial intelligence technologies—we should stop and think to ourselves if the bad outweighs the good, the harm it could cause others and reflect on how to we can protect, even if it goes against our bottom line.

Unlike the realities of our economic system, which rewards growth in capital regardless of any ethical or moral consequences. If we create solely to belong within that climate then we shed our responsibility and fail our world which depends on creators to act on their ideas for the sake of creation while being able to abstain for the sake of the greater good.

To our industry - sobriety

It's a miracle whenever any video game project is released, it's even more of a miracle when it's also a video game that garners a level of success (however you may gauge that). In some cases, especially in large-scale productions, hundreds of people come together for years to make the project a reality. Hundreds of people with different life journeys and inspiration coming together to work on a highly collaborative endeavor with one product to show for at the end of it. The developers will be pouring days of their lives that they'll never get back, losing time with loved ones and in some cases unfortunately even sleep towards that ultimate goal, of sending a game out to the world that will touch people's lives, and generate enough revenue to sustain them and their companies to hopefully make another one.

In the face of all of this, we as creative leaders hold a responsibility to ourselves, those people who work with us and to the industry at large to exercise creative sobriety. I would urge all of you to consider and ponder on those questions:

- Are we able to articulate why we are making the creative decisions we are making?
- Are the foundations of this project a group of inevitable ideas?
- How can we intellectually push our ideas further towards originality?
- Are we blinded by parts of our life journey that we take feedback as a personal attack?
- Is our frustration when others don't understand our vision a fault of their own or our ability to articulate that vision?
- How can we articulate that vision better?
- Are we really serving those we are leading?
- Are we being vulnerable and authentic in how we are creating?
- Are making games inspired by how the world is touching us?
- Are we being courageous enough to stand for our project and our team in the face of fear and uncertainty?
- Are we aware of our own creative dilemma?
- Are we getting enough feedback along the way to make sure our creative dilemma is updated with the right information along the way?

Some readers might've thought that the language of this book has changed from tackling the subject of creativity philosophy, to neuroscience, to sociology, to design to even business. I tried my best to showcase the different aspects that are to be present in our minds as we tackle creativity in our field and the layers of responsibility that are affected by that awareness.

Creativity in society

There's a dynamic relationship between the individual and the collective. Ideas—as we showcased in Chapter 5—can be refined, challenged, and improved within a setting of a community. No creator truly exists in isolation, they're always part of a greater society around them that influences them through environment, culture, history, and interactions with peers.

Society on its own is also a source of inspiration. As creators contemplate their own societies and accepted norms. They seek to present it with their craft or challenge it. Throughout history, societies have viewed those creations back and other nurtured or stifled the creative output. Societies that champion free thought, encourage questioning, and appreciate diversity become hubs for artistic, scientific, and creative innovations. Conversely, societies that enforce rigid conformity, suppress dissent, and prioritize dogma over curiosity tend to stifle creative spirits. Yet, the creative spirit triumphs in both, as the act of creation not only becomes an artistic or an intellectual endeavor but also a statement of political or moral value.

It's a symbiotic relationship between the creator and their environment. Oftentimes, societies resist groundbreaking ideas or radical expressions, in the same way Monet was part of the refused, as himself and creators generally tend to challenge the established norms or beliefs. However, as we've seen in countless examples of this book starting with the impressionists, creativity thrives in that tension. The resistance, the challenges, and the breakthroughs define the evolution of both individuals and civilizations.

This adds to the responsibilities of the creator to reflect on their own society in their work. Reflecting on the ethical dimension of creation in the value added of the creative journey they're about to embark on and the statement they want to make. Every creative act holds a statement, we need to ponder its true meaning to us as we're making it. Understanding that, and how it relates to our society—local or global—is also us practicing creative sobriety.

What we create can be transformative. It has the power to stir and invoke introspection. It has the ability to transport individuals to different realms of consciousness. Our creations can offer glimpses into alternate realities, perspectives, and emotions. We invite the players—and viewers alike—to partake in our visions, feel our emotions that we're expressing vulnerably and reflect upon their own experiences and beliefs.

Future of creativity

Our modern times are busy ones. We spoke about the pace of technical innovation in Chapter 4 that is going on at an unprecedented pace in human history, an overwhelming influx of information and a rapidly shifting of societal norms and values play a huge role in shaping—and sometimes hindering—our creative processes.

Originality is challenged in an age where vast amounts of content are produced every moment. A challenge of depth in an era of fleeting attention spans and the challenge of authenticity in a time that is dominated by curated personas and virtual realities.

The rise of artificial intelligence and its sophisticated capabilities to produce creative work that once was the monopoly of mankind. Increasing the output of content on those curated channels, man can not outmatch the machine when it comes to the quantity of output.

It is in the face of these challenges more than ever that we need to exercise creative sobriety. The inevitable ideas that we discussed in Chapter 3 will soon become the job of the machine. This is where creative sobriety is crucial. Creators need to hold tighter to what makes us unique. Our authenticity and reflection, our representation of the uniqueness of our life journey is something I believe a machine can't simulate. AI can only produce variations of what's already been made. The translation of how the world touches us in a unique way, our perspectives and introspections of our personal life journeys is what makes us truly unique. It is what will make us stand out in the floods of mass produced content of the machines.

Parting words

The need to create is fundamental to our humanity; that's our nature, which will never change, though it might take different forms.

Our sobriety, however, is our creative refuge. Diving through what makes us truly unique, our individual and collective human experience, it's our sure path to originality in the face of all challenges.

It's been within us the whole time.

Further Reading

Brown, R. M. (2011). *Starting from Scratch: A Different Kind of Writers' Manual*. Bantam.
Fromm, E. (2013). *The art of being*. Open Road Media.

Ivory, J. D.& Kowert, R & Quandt, T (2015). A brief history of video games. In *The video game debate*. Routledge. Pp. 1–21

Maté, G. (2022). *The myth of normal: Trauma, illness and healing in a toxic culture*. Knopf Canada.

May, R. (1994). *The courage to create*. WW Norton & Company.

Mayer, J (2006). *Slow Dancing in a Burning Room*. [Recorded by John Mayer]. On Continuum. Columbia Records.

Nietzsche, F., & Hollingdale, R.J. (2020). *Thus spoke Zarathustra*. Routledge.

Index

Note: **Bold** page numbers refer to tables and *italic* page numbers refer to figures.

Printed in the United States
by Baker & Taylor Publisher Services